PROTEST T-SHIRTS

Graffito Books
32 Great Sutton Street
Clerkenwell
London
EC1V 0NB
UK

www.graffitobooks.com

General Editor: Eleanor Mathieson
Production: Yak El-Droubie

With special thanks to Lindsey Edwards and Helen Edwards

Printed in Portugal

ISBN: 978-0-9553398-9-9
British Library cataloguing-in-publication data
A catalogue record of this book is available at the British Library

PROTEST T-SHIRTS

DESIGNS FROM THE CULT INDEPENDENTS

GRAFFITO
www.graffitobooks.com

CONTENTS

THE INDEPENDENT SCENE

The t-shirt is unique in fashion terms – cheap, always fashionable, classless, globally recognized, available everywhere, a blank canvas waiting to be filled. Independent thinkers and designers are capitalizing on its ability to transcend boundaries and carry their subversive, controversial messages or provocations. It has become a piece of independent media which can infiltrate spaces where activists cannot usually make their point. Find a design and message that resonates with you and you can put a shirt on, walk down the street and let people know what's going on in your head.

Whether hand-printed as one-off designs or created using mass-production methods, the shirts produced by the companies featured here have a lot in common with street art. Both have been used as a way of getting anti-establishment views into public places. They use a similar visual language, often resulting in a type of anti-advertising – a subverted version of recognizable concepts or brands, just as witty as the mainstream in using irony and visual juxtaposition to make an idea stick. The issues covered here are as numerous as the designers who bring them to our attention – the oil wars going on in the Middle East, the transformation of the U.S. into a surveillance society, the worship of brands, the destruction of the environment, the lies of the media, the climate of fear used to control the West, the heritage of the civil rights movement, the god-like influence of celebrity – and there are a myriad of ways in which these issues are approached. Some designers go for bold, straight-faced and searingly direct slogans, others have a more eccentric, surreal response to their targets, producing designs that are tangential, and refreshingly hilarious.

The democratizing effect of the internet means that previously sidelined voices and small start-up companies now have a way of distributing and selling their shirts worldwide. There has been an explosion of activity as a result of this, with a vibrant independent t-shirt scene springing up in the last few years. The appeal of designs from those working at the edge of fashion is huge – these clothes have a story behind them – produced by real people, conceptualized by small creative design teams. The labels are an alternative to branded fashion; people increasingly want to wear independently created, rare and limited-edition designs.

Can a slogan change the world? Or is it enough to make people think? The public have been willing to wear and advertise brand names for years; now the independents are hijacking a desire to wear good design to showcase the issues they want to promote or confront. As a result, those who are buying the shirts are doing more than getting dressed in the morning – they are using their bodies to stimulate debate, amuse, turn heads and minds.

SEEE

'I WANT MY NATURE BACK'

A SHIRT FROM SEEE'S REVOLUTION COLLECTION

THE HENLEY COLLEGE LIBRARY

Jennifer Garcia named her company Star Electric Eighty Eight (SEEE), after her favorite jersey (worn by an electrician's baseball league team). Based in Harlem, N.Y.C., SEEE launched their first designs in 2004. They produce an annual, limited-edition collection, featuring tees, zine and print. Previous years have addressed consumerism, religion, prescription drug abuse and the concept of self-help.

SEEE have been featured in the *New York Times*, on Josh Rubin's Coolhunting website and in the "To A Tee" exhibit at Atlanta's Museum of Design (MODA). **>>**

'NI DIEU NI MAÎTRE' (NEITHER GOD NOR MASTER)

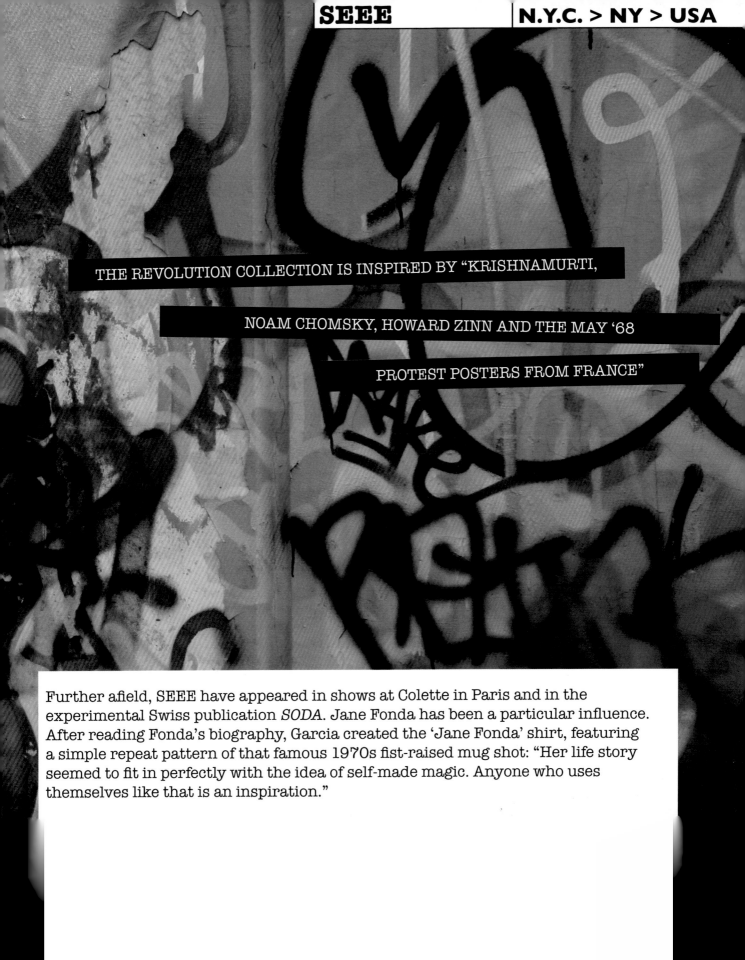

THE REVOLUTION COLLECTION IS INSPIRED BY "KRISHNAMURTI,

NOAM CHOMSKY, HOWARD ZINN AND THE MAY '68

PROTEST POSTERS FROM FRANCE"

Further afield, SEEE have appeared in shows at Colette in Paris and in the experimental Swiss publication *SODA*. Jane Fonda has been a particular influence. After reading Fonda's biography, Garcia created the 'Jane Fonda' shirt, featuring a simple repeat pattern of that famous 1970s fist-raised mug shot: "Her life story seemed to fit in perfectly with the idea of self-made magic. Anyone who uses themselves like that is an inspiration."

THE GRAPHIC PATTERN ON THIS SHIRT IS MADE UP OF IMAGES OF

POLITICAL ACTIVIST AND AEROBICS QUEEN JANE FONDA

FONDA WAS DUBBED "HANOI JANE"

DUE TO HER ANTI-VIETNAM WAR PROTESTS

13

'DEATH TO TRADITION'

'NO WAR': THE GUN SHOOTS

FLOWERS, NOT BULLETS

THE LOVE MOVEMENT

'WHAT IF SADDAM SKATED?'

"Do Good, Feel Good" is the mantra of L.A.-based The Love Movement (TLM). Established three years ago, the group is a collaboration between designers, artists, teachers, and architects. The shirts featured here are from TLM's collaboration with Ropeadope.

Producing public art and gallery shows, TLM create pieces that critique and poke fun at society and pop culture, while drawing attention to international affairs. What have they focused on recently? – "the Iraq War, instability in the Middle East, human rights violations in China, the genocide in Darfur...and the understanding that underneath it all, we are all the same."

TLM like using discarded materials for their art: "we like the idea of creating beauty from the stuff society has thought is worthless." They follow up their cultural commentary with action, recently helping to establish a fresh water well in Benin, Africa, with profits from the sale of their art. Their collaborations with the Peace Corps and the International Humanity Foundation have helped to provide schooling for children in Benin and Bali, Indonesia.

'SAME UNDERNEATH'

MORE SHIRTS FROM THE COLLABORATION WITH ROPEADOPE

'TANK EYES': A VIEW THROUGH THE SIGHTS

OF A TANK, READY TO SHOOT

MAAK EEBUH

A SHIRT FROM MAAK EEBUH'S WAR SERIES

After working in high-end fashion and costume design at Yigal Azrouel, Harlem-based Jade Schulz started her limited edition t-shirt line and brand "to filter important issues of the moment in a different light." She is happy to provoke with clever visual ambiguity and language tricks. In her 'War Series' line, Middle-Eastern eyes, with heavy kohl makeup, gaze through a tank viewing-slit as if through a yashmak. Another design uses old-world graphics with the words "American Empyre", a suggestion that, however powerful, all empires fade and become history in the end.

'PUPPETS OF LUXURY': PARIS HILTON, KARL LAGERFELD, P DIDDY

THE 'RIOTS' SHIRT: A MARTIN LUTHER KING QUOTE

Freshjive founder Rick Klotz cut his teeth designing flyers for some of the club and music scenes bubbling in the L.A. area during the mid to late eighties. In 1989, Rick switched from paper to cloth and Freshjive was born. Thoroughly rooted in L.A. culture, Freshjive drew inspiration early on from hip hop, punk, surf, skate and art, and then mixed these influences with some sharp political and social commentary.

>>

The latter has generated considerable controversy. Freshjive's t-shirt 'Victimized' was trying to draw attention to the plight of Palestinian children, drawn into the conflict in the Middle East as soldiers (whether the blame lies with Palestinian parents or the Israeli military is not specified). Klotz was accused of creating a "Jew-hating t-shirt" in one blog.

His defence was vigorous "it's one of the highest purposes of art to spark discussion by getting people to think about serious issues...I am certainly not Jew-hating...there are victims on all sides of the conflict and I have the right to make this statement...discussions from both sides of the fence are essential for real understanding."

>>

FRESHJIVE'S CONTROVERSIAL 'VICTIMIZED' SHIRT DRAWS ATTENTION TO THE MILITARIZATION OF SOME PALESTINIAN CHILDREN

'REVOLUTIONARY SUICIDE'

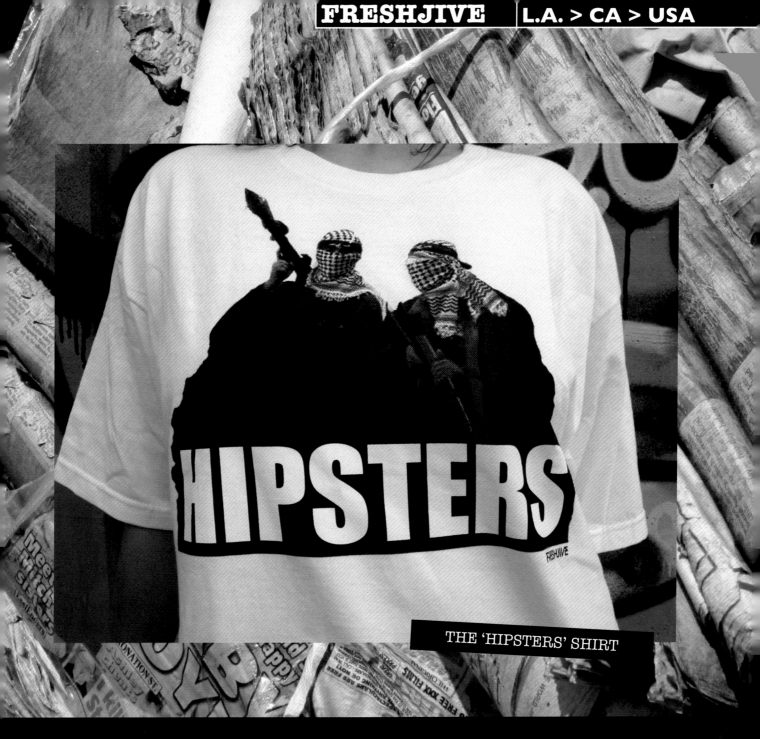

THE 'HIPSTERS' SHIRT

Whilst Klotz wants people to buy his t-shirts for their message, as well as for aesthetic or fashion reasons, the shirts look great and are suffused with edgy humor. One shows a couple of Mujahadeen as hipsters, another a hot porn star masturbating (seemingly in the minds of a couple of bored US soldiers of Vietnam vintage). "Party in Iraq" is spelled out in a design that seems to be a sardonic comment on the disastrous situation there. The 'Decadence' shirt, shows Bush, Rice and Rumsfeld in Nazi and S&M gear, with a White House in the background looking rather like the Berlin Reichstag. It is clear that controversy has not dented Klotz's desire to create thought-provoking and visceral t-shirt designs.

'WAR, WOMEN, WAVES' DETAIL

THE 'WAR, WOMEN, WAVES' SHIRT

THE LETTERS PICKED OUT OF THE KEFFIYEH-STYLE

PATTERN READ 'PARTY IN IRAQ'

'DECADENCE': A HELL-LIKE VIEW OF THE BUSH

ADMINISTRATION

THE LOOTS

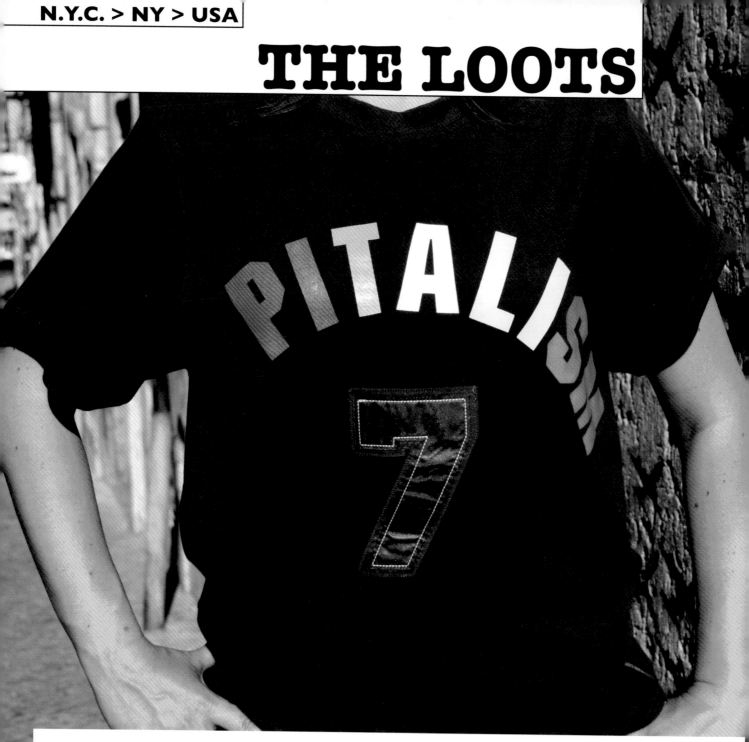

The Loots describe themselves as "a really tight group." They relish the design freedom being an independent company brings: "in the past we worked and designed for other companies. When it's your own you have the freedom to design what you like, not what you're told to like."

The 'Capitalism' shirt is a take-off of a sports jersey, backing the team that always wins. This tongue-in-cheek humor is paired with a practical attempt at change: The Loots support the Tikva charity, which funds an orphanage in the Ukraine. "Sure the money's important, but, without wanting to sound corny, money is made and lost, but people never forget a kind word or a quick smile."

THE 'CAPITALISM' SHIRT

THE BACK READS: RICH GET RICHER

SHIRT WITH GOLD KISER LOGO

KISER

THE LOGO, TWO CROSSED AK-47'S AND A FLOWER, REPRESENTS THE

CONCEPT BEHIND THE KISER LINE: HUNT BEAUTY

THE 'SOLE REBEL' SHIRT

Kiser Haydar Barnes started selling his t-shirt designs on the streets of Soho N.Y.C. in 2004. The limited edition tees (displayed on an ironing board) caught the attention of boutique owners and fashion editors, and the brand has now grown to be recognized and sold internationally, while maintaining its independence and graphic style.

This design style is clearly influenced by Kiser's background – born of American parents in Nigeria, he went to High School in Israel, before studying graphic design at Rochester Institute of Technology. His designs draw on both African and Middle-Eastern iconography, which adds a multicultural dimension to the brand's recurring themes: the hunt for beauty and the search for peace.

>>

'NEVER DO WHAT THEY DO'

'SOLE REBEL' SHIRT: THE SLOGAN IS STYLED IN ARABIC-INFLUENCED LETTERING

KISER explain that "the brand is built around the concept of 'A Graphic Life': the dedication to live in a creatively explicit manner. This theme is present throughout the brand and in our collaborations as well. We like to keep a balance of intellectual designs and playful themes. Sometimes we focus on political issues like the war in Iraq, and sometimes we create designs that are strictly for fun."

When asked what sets them apart from bigger companies/brands, the distinction is simple: "our work tends to start off as art and then make its way into a commercial form, versus many brands who start off with a commercial idea then try to make it creative."

MORE ARABIC-INFLUENCED LETTERING

ON THIS 'PEACE' SHIRT

'THE END UP' SHIRT

YOU WORK FOR THEM

THE TEXT ON THE SHIRT INCLUDES A QUOTE FROM FRANK B.KELLOGG (NOBEL PEACE PRIZE WINNER)WHICH READS: "I BELIEVE THAT IN THE END, THE ABOLITION OF WAR, THE MAINTENENCE OF WORLD PEACE, THE ADJUSTMENT OF INTERNATIONAL QUESTIONS BY PACIFIC MEANS, WILL COME THROUGH THE FORCE OF PUBLIC OPINION, WHICH CONTROLS NATIONS AND PEOPLES".

Focused on selling to designers and the design-aware, You Work For Them own their own shop and can therefore curate their space – "we only stock the stuff that we would wear." Founded by Michael Cina and Michael Young in 2001, the company's limited edition shirts have very short runs, allowing them to create shirts which reflect their current concerns, but which they hope transcend short-term fashion. "We focus on human-related issues – stuff that we happen to be thinking about or are interested in." This has included supporting social causes such as a homeless shelter in Minneapolis, but also international disaster relief.

YOUNG LOVERS

THE 'GUNS AND ARMS' SHIRT

"THESE ARMS CAN KILL"

Founded in 2005 by Finnish-Australian designer Luke Nuto, Young Lovers rejects temporary fashion trends in order to create classics – "we want our shirts to look even better 10 years from now – as you look back to the swirling nights from which they came." Every shirt is strictly limited to a run of 100. The inspiration for the label comes from "the intersection of art and music, twilight and midnight...we celebrate the madness of midnight love and all that surrounds it." Declaring "opposition to the movements of the un-radical majority," their designs use visual and verbal puns, or directly reference musical influences.

LYRICS FROM VANILLA ICE'S "ICE ICE BABY"

'ARAB'

'GAZA STRIP CLUB'

$cientology
Out of
L.A.

'SCIENTOLOGY OUT OF L.A.'

DANGEROUS BREED

'IRAQ'

Subversive wit, subtle and ironic design, where the message comes across, but doesn't "scream...in plain ugly, unwearable fashion": all of these things characterize Dangerous Breed's designs. Describing themselves as "an accidental t-shirt company" they sprang up with their hit 'Jesus hates your S.U.V.' shirt.

Dangerous Breed have found a rich vein in hijacking the cliché of the holiday t-shirt to brilliant ends. 'Iraq' with a tropical beach scene, the unlikely 'Ski Iraq' and 'Gaza Strip Club' are great examples.

>>

Sometimes the current social and political climate serves their ends, as in the simple 'Arab', challenging the viewer's racial assumptions in a post 9/11 world.

Allusions to all-American brands allow a deeper message to be conveyed – 'Khartoum Network' makes you pause and think before you get the connection between Darfur and Chinese support for the Sudanese government conducting the genocide. 'Guantanamo!' is a more direct case in point, sardonically pointing out the iniquity of the Bush White House project there. "We hope to call attention to the disparity between the self-absorption of consumerist society and the desperate need for responsible dialogue in an increasingly global community."

Dangerous Breed also aim to do this "without shouting out hackneyed messages...we want to start conversations, not end them."

'GUANTANAMO!'

'SKI IRAQ'

'BEIRUT 40K MARATHON'

'KHARTOUM NETWORK'

Northern California label Tonic Generation have taken social action through t-shirt sales to a whole new level, and their shirts carry the message loud and clear. Harnessing the purchasing power of US consumers allows them to do good in direct ways: "You can support one great teacher...Inderjit Khurana...with one great t-shirt. This amazing woman has brought school to needy children who have been forced to live around the railway platforms of Bhubhaneshwar, India." By including a statement of where the money is going on the back of the shirt, the

EVERY COUNTS

THE 'NET' SHIRT

TEXT ON THE BACK OF THE SHIRT READS: "THIS SHIRT HAS PROVIDED 3

MOSQUITO BED NETS IN AFRICA"

MAMA

OPERATION: SAIGON SUNSET

"Integrity, honesty and beauty" are the principles behind San Francisco-based Mama, one of the few women's streetwear lines designed and run by a woman, Gabriella Davi-Khorasanee. In running her one-woman show, Davi-Khorasanee has been helping "ladies look fly" since 2004.

The themes behind Mama's collections change seasonally and the 1960s provide a strong visual direction for the collection featured here, with the visual iconography of that time used to highlight current concerns. Davi-Khorasanee says: "My collection 'Operation: Saigon Sunset' identifies similarities between the unwanted war in Vietnam and our current unwanted war in Iraq."

>>

'ALL YOU NEED IS DRUGS'

THE 'IMAGINE' SHIRT: LYRICS FROM JOHN LENNON'S CLASSIC PEACE SO

'DRAGON' SHIRT WITH "MAMA" ON THE ARMS

'MAKE LOVE NOT WAR'

'SGT. PEPPER' SHIRTS

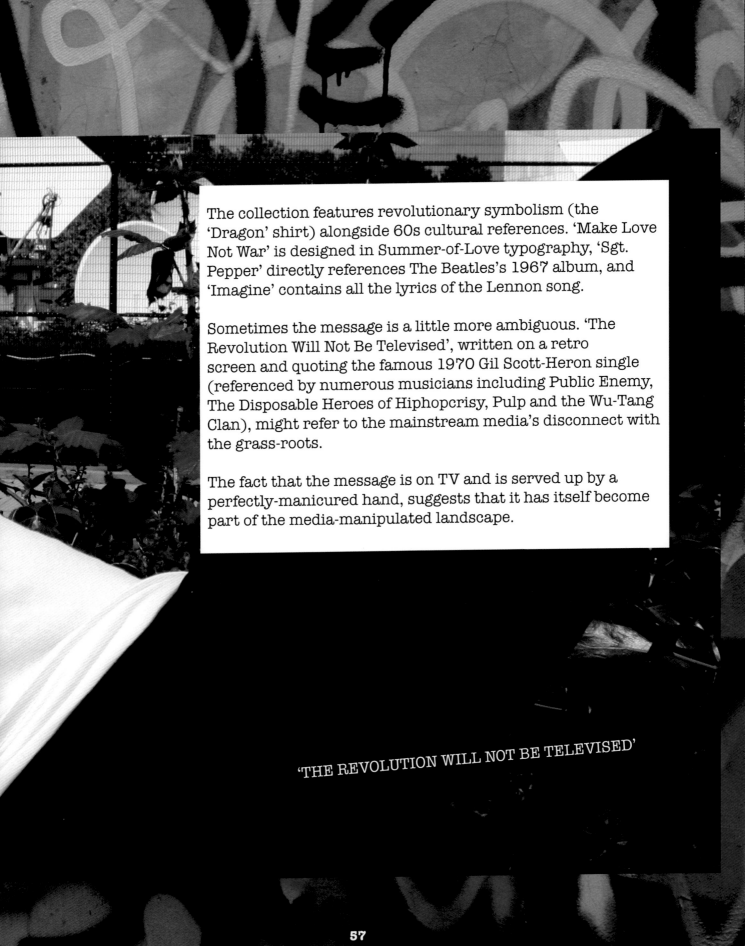

The collection features revolutionary symbolism (the 'Dragon' shirt) alongside 60s cultural references. 'Make Love Not War' is designed in Summer-of-Love typography, 'Sgt. Pepper' directly references The Beatles's 1967 album, and 'Imagine' contains all the lyrics of the Lennon song.

Sometimes the message is a little more ambiguous. 'The Revolution Will Not Be Televised', written on a retro screen and quoting the famous 1970 Gil Scott-Heron single (referenced by numerous musicians including Public Enemy, The Disposable Heroes of Hiphopcrisy, Pulp and the Wu-Tang Clan), might refer to the mainstream media's disconnect with the grass-roots.

The fact that the message is on TV and is served up by a perfectly-manicured hand, suggests that it has itself become part of the media-manipulated landscape.

'THE REVOLUTION WILL NOT BE TELEVISED'

SHIRTS FROM BRIAN WOOD'S AFRICAN WARLORD COLLECTION

Brian Wood says that his aim is to create clothing that allows men to dress better than women. Since launching Brian Wood Exclusive in 2003, with a pop art-influenced hand-painted t-shirt collection, he has expanded into cut and sew men's sportswear with his label Brian Wood. This original pop sentiment can still be seen in the Brian Wood Exclusive, hyper-colorful, politically and socially-aware, t-shirt designs. Wood, who designs, produces, sells and pitches to fashion magazines from his N.Y.C. studio, wants to "provoke, but in a way that makes people think."

His 'African Warlord '08' collection includes shirts which comment on the global domination of corporations; they feature a colorful African continent emblazoned with Western brands. Wood also makes use of the Black Power salute, decorating it with traditional African textile designs

MADE IN U.S.A.

GOOD

CLASS

U.S. BRAND LOGOS MIXED UP IN THE SHAPE OF THE AFRICAN CONTINENT

'THREE FISTS'

One t-shirt features a Nissan pick-up truck (standard transport in Africa) with guns spilling out of it – a reference to the arms trade. His eye for detail extends to the packaging for the shirts: plastic specimen bags featuring bright red biohazard warnings.

Brian Wood supports a number of causes related to HIV/AIDS in Africa, and projects which aim to get inner-city kids interested in creativity before they're tempted to switch to crime. "It's so important to engage with the kids early" he says.

'COKA-COOLA'

BRIAN WOOD PACKAGING

THIS SHIRT FEATURES FABRICS PRINTED WITH

DIFFERENT BRAND LOGOS CUT UP AND STITCHED BACK TOGETHER

LEFT: NELSON MANDELA, MUHAMMAD ALI AND

DESMOND TUTU ALL FEATURE ON THIS SHIRT

PEACE IS A DISEASE, MEET THE CURE...

2 SICK BASTARDS X

...SEXING UP THE WAR ON TERROR

TRANS-GENDER WARFARE IN GUT-WRENCHING TECHNICOLOR!

2SB GRAPHIC SCENES

WARNING: SOME SCENES OF VIOLENCE
MAY BE CONSIDERED EXTREMELY EROTIC

2SICKBASTARDS

'JUST DO IT – YOU LITTLE BASTARD'

Self-deprecating and satirical to a caustic degree, 2SB don't mince words. They describe themselves as "purveyors of quality shit"; their blog is entitled 'Smut, Snuff and Scum'; once in, in a take on the Nike strapline, they state "We are not you, we're not just doin' it, we're not lovin' it and we are not the real thing...we create artwork, design t-shirts and generally make money out of other people's misery."

The boys behind the brand, Ben and Sam, kicked off in 2002 with street stencils (an early version of their 'George4Saddam' design), released a range of hand-stencilled tees and put on an art exhibition in Soho, London with FACT magazine.

>>

SADDAM AND BUSH: 2SICKBASTARDS

2SICKBASTARDS

'XXXTREMIST'

PUTTING THE FUN BACK INTO FUNDAMENTALISM

'SKULL FUCKER'

THE SKULL IS ENTIRELY MADE UP OF LOGOS

Initially, everything was produced in their kitchen (including hand stamping the swingtags and sewing in the neck labels) but as demand has grown they have switched to screen-printing, at Transformer in East London.

Their sardonic humor shines through every design: George W and Saddam french-kissing, Britney and Christina enjoying double-ended fun, and Kate Moss suffering the side-effects of enjoying too much 'cola'. The new range will include several notorious dictators as well as Amy Winehouse.

Their influences? "Exploitation and B-movies, Hunter S. Thompson, Jack Kerouac, Charles Bukowski, underground magazines, Robert Crumb, Chris Morris, comic-books, album covers, sub-cultures, punk, heavy metal, Andy Warhol, Roy Lichtenstein, Salvador Dali and Shepard Fairey, amongst others." Quite a brew. In 2009 they mount a retrospective of their work.

SUCK ON THIS: CHARLTON HESTON

2SICKBASTARDS

SOCIAL ATELIER

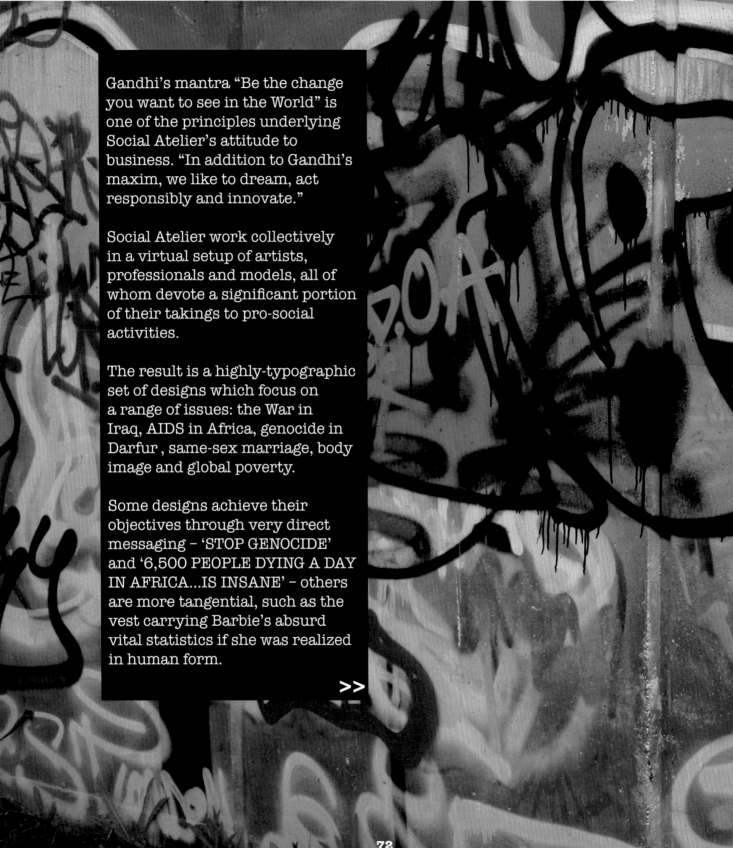

Gandhi's mantra "Be the change you want to see in the World" is one of the principles underlying Social Atelier's attitude to business. "In addition to Gandhi's maxim, we like to dream, act responsibly and innovate."

Social Atelier work collectively in a virtual setup of artists, professionals and models, all of whom devote a significant portion of their takings to pro-social activities.

The result is a highly-typographic set of designs which focus on a range of issues: the War in Iraq, AIDS in Africa, genocide in Darfur , same-sex marriage, body image and global poverty.

Some designs achieve their objectives through very direct messaging – 'STOP GENOCIDE' and '6,500 PEOPLE DYING A DAY IN AFRICA...IS INSANE' – others are more tangential, such as the vest carrying Barbie's absurd vital statistics if she was realized in human form.

>>

'SAME LOVE ONE STATE'

IN 2004 MASSACHUSETTS BECAME THE FIRST AND ONLY

U.S. STATE TO LEGALISE SAME-SEX MARRIAGE

'STOP GENOCIDE': SOCIAL ATELIER HAVE FOCUSED ON THE

THIS SHIRT LISTS THE

VITAL STATISTICS OF EVERY GIRL'S

FASHION IDOL: BARBIE

39"
19"
33"

TEXT READS: '6,500 PEOPLE DYING A DAY

IN AFRICA OF A PREVENTABLE

DISEASE IS INSANE'

SOCIAL ATELIER WANT TO "STAND UP AND SPEAK FOR THOSE WHO HAVE NO VOICE"

RIGHT: THIS SHIRT WAS LAUNCHED ON

THE EVE OF THE WAR WITH IRAQ

Social Atelier have a long history of collaboration with bodies such as CARE, the Solar Cooker Project for Darfur, and Rock The Vote (they were exclusive 2008 apparel licensees). "We try to go just beyond financial contributions however, by raising awareness within the fashion and thought-leader communities."

The t-shirts bring a high-end fashion feel to activism, unsurprising given that Social Atelier's founders, Andrei Najjar and Ya'el Āfriat have collectively worked for the big hitters of the US fashion world – Abercrombie & Fitch, Hollister, Gap, Banana Republic and Urban Outfitters.

The word 'truth' is vital to the brand; they print stark statistics or slogans in simple neutral colours, asking their customers to act as human billboards. As their manifesto states: "we use sleek, cutting edge fashion as the most personal medium to communicate the unbiased truth."

THE HENLEY COLLEGE LIBRARY

RNDM

'FUCK GUNS'

Stockholm-based RNDM are a small brand that started producing shirts in 2002. They are not interested in getting rich from the business, and say "For us it's enough just to see you out there in the city, wearing our clothes."

"We like to be seen as a company that makes clothes that shine through with a feeling or a clear message. More of an eye/feeling opener other than 'Just another T-shirt.'" They've certainly achieved that ambition with 'Fuck Guns', which achieves its effect through a seriously provocative image, which would make people look twice in the street.

SPRAYGRAPHIC

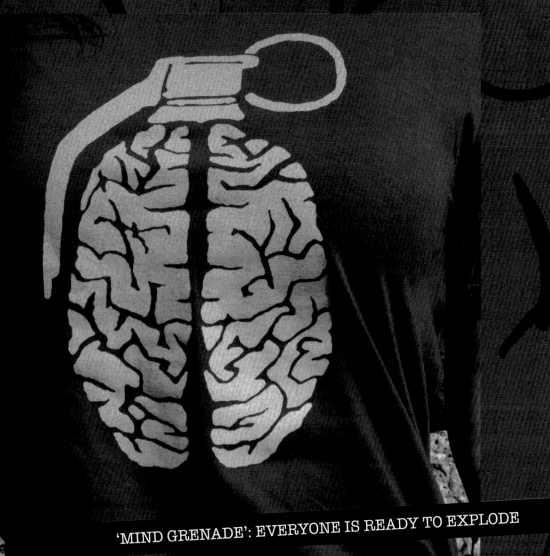

'MIND GRENADE': EVERYONE IS READY TO EXPLODE

The massive expansion of surveillance in the USA and Europe is a major concern for Spraygraphic Apparel's founders Chuck Banaszewski, Ph.D and Matt Krise. After graduating in theatre from Arizona State University, Chuck B founded the Arizona Surveillance Camera Players. "My goal is to try and get people to think more about art, pop culture, symbols and materialism without telling people the answer; I want to provoke thought...and the t-shirt is such a unique and popular medium for doing this...it's a way of making people think more about life in general." Spraygraphic.com is now a creative community, which allows artists, designers, filmmakers, musicians and activists to upload and share their work by creating an online portfolio.

'PEEPING TOM': BIG BROTHER IS WATCHING

GORILLA RIOT

THE 'SHOE TRIBE' SHIRT: SPOT THE BRANDS

Gorilla Riot was created by Kyle Cross and Nick Black in 2006. Kyle had already co-founded Digital Three, a collection of rebellious young artists, which quickly became a Sarasota design institution and a magnet for creatives from the skate, punk and hip-hop scenes. Kyle's concept for Gorilla Riot was to have an artist-driven clothing label: " I wanted Gorilla Riot to be 'filterless'; a place where nothing is taboo; a global soap-box" he explains.

The company operates almost like an art gallery. T-shirts are made in very limited editions of 50 and feature work by guest artists and designers. The company has a green mindset: they are "always looking for the most environmentally-friendly approach."

>>

THE 'KNIGHT' SHIRT

A TRIBAL MASK CREATED USING BRAND SYMBOLS

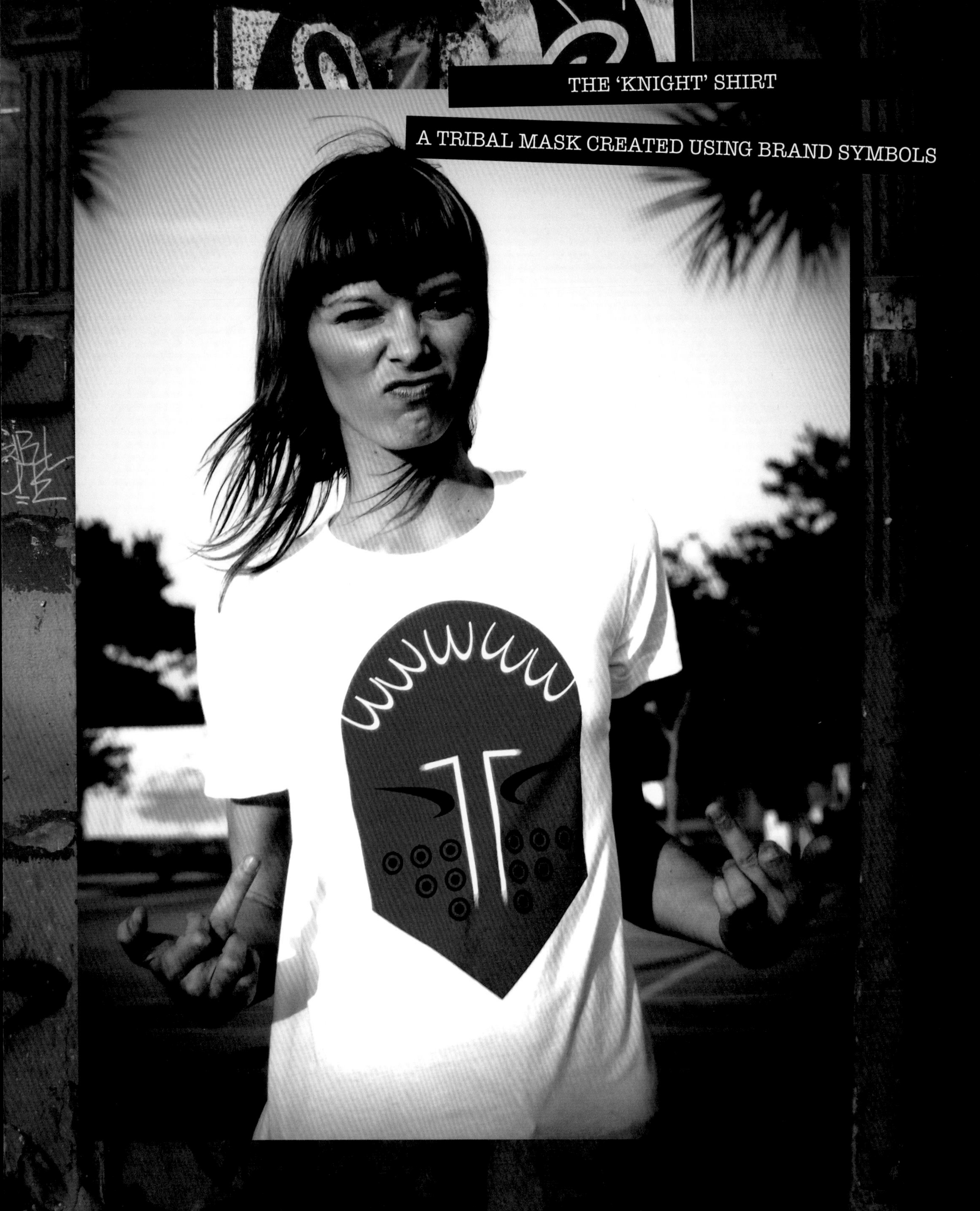

'SAMURAI BRAND'

The creative energy of the work stands out: the 'Art of Visual Warfare' range (designed by Digital Three) references corporate logos, combining them to look like masks or primitive symbols of war. The 'History 101' set, designed by Kyle Cross and Matt Morris (a.k.a. Coolvader) features seemingly ancient screen printed mugshots of assassinated presidents, with detailed depictions of the murder weapons on the back. Gorilla Riot's most recent project is Store 101, a unique designer boutique and art gallery in Gainesville, FL, featuring their work, alongside that of their many collaborators. The store came about because "we wanted a deliberate throw-back to traditional shopping."

'GAS GUZZLER': ANOTHER SHIRT FROM THE

ART OF VISUAL WARFARE COLLECTION

'LINCOLN' SHIRT FROM THE HISTORY 101 COLLECTION

6 INCH DERRINGER

6 INCH DERRINGER: THE GUN THAT WAS USED TO ASSASSINATE LINCOLN

IT IS OFFICIALLY ACCEPTED THAT JFK WAS ASSASSINATED BY

A MANNLICHER -CARCANO RIFLE

'JFK' SHIRT

HISTORY 101

MANNLICHER – CARCANO

BACK PRINT FROM 'LINCOLN' SHIRT

BACK PRINT FROM 'JFK' SHIRT

HISTORY 101

POP VULTURE T-SHIRT

Pop Vulture is the almost ironic name for the L.A.-based studio whose most consistent motif is the dove of peace. The company has been hugely preoccupied with the iniquities of the Iraq War, with designs that have an almost 1960s straightforward desire for peace. The t-shirt 'World Peace One' asks the simple question, what if the U.S. chose to drop doves of peace rather than bombs?

'WORLD PEACE ONE'

BIRDHEAD DESIGN

'NO MORE WAR'

Founder Michael Crigler created Birdhead in 2000 whilst living in Japan. It started out as a one-man show making limited edition shirts and accessories. "Our goal was to merge the gap between art and fashion, providing alternatives to cookie-cutter mainstream fashion brands." The brand now also produces posters, stationery and books, but the t-shirts remain key: "there is no other art form that is more personal than fashion." Some of Birdhead's designs have an undercurrent of macabre humor, as in the logo-like 'No More War', while the unremittingly gloomy 'Man Will Destroy Man', sends a message of environmental as well as racial violence.

'MESS WITH TEXAS'

STREET ATTACK

MESSWITHTEXAS.COM IS A PROGRESSIVE ACTION BLOG

Street Attack takes many forms – a clothing company, marketing agency, design agency, fashion/lifestyle brand and a social mission rolled into one. The latter is central to their thinking: "We believe in local materials, local production and proper labor practices...and that everyone can live a lifestyle that does not use resources derived from animals." Most of the company is vegan or vegetarian: it's all about reducing human impact as much as possible. Their designs feature mostly social and moral issues "but always with humor, sarcasm and insight." The ironic, anti-Bush 'Mess With Texas', is the name of a progressive action blog set up by the company.

DISTRICT COTTON

'BIKES NOT BOMBS' SHIRT

N.Y.C.-based District Cotton is scathing of companies who 'green-wash' their businesses: "we believe that you have to build up from core principles – when we built the company we placed labor and environmental concerns at the heart of what we do." Their t-shirts bear out this philosophy – pared down designs with the optimism that green solutions and collective action will win the day, eloquently expressed by designs such as the huge 'bike fish', seen here easily swallowing a Hummer.

VANGUARD AMERICAN

FREE EARTH

THE 'FREE EARTH' SHIRT

Vanguard American started life as a video project in 2003 and evolved into a t-shirt company; recently they have spawned a witty furniture line (their 'Moss Table' features live moss and a built-in mirror for efficient coke-snorting). Their designs, whilst having a deep vein of humor, are a direct reaction to the politics of Bush-era USA: "politically, our freedoms are being limited, democratic representation is being distorted, and complacency is now the norm...our t-shirts address these issues." Vanguard American's designs always have an interesting angle; 'Free Earth' is a succinct expression of the benefits of wind power – free to generate and free from the political oppression of the oil lobby; their 'CHAD Ruined My Life' shirt a reference to

>>

FREE EARTH

BEST WORN WITH NO PANTS

the flawed ballot-accounting system employed in Florida in the 2004 Presidential elections; 'Deer World' alludes to Bush's compromised grammar and lack of sincerity. You can order their t-shirts with optional bullet-holes "created by real rednecks;" should you think this is just a joke, their website features a video of rednecks shooting the shirts, clearly enjoying themselves. One declares "this is the American dream, baby."

Vanguard American t-shirts come only in black and every shirt includes a "freshness indicator logo" under the right armpit, so if you don't wash, your t-shirt will know first.

think outside

THE 'THINK OUTSIDE' SHIRT

'CHAD RUINED MY LIFE'

'DEER WORLD, I'M SORRY'

NEW INTERNATIONALIST

'NO FUEL TANK' SHIRT

no fuel tank
no emissions
no oil wars
no regrets

A campaigning communications co-operative, New Internationalist has been publishing its renowned magazine for over 30 years and has 75,000 subscribers globally. The issues they highlight are broad-ranging, from the abuse of human rights in Burma to the 8,000 executed in China each year, the breach of environmental promises in the West, and the effects of the arms trade in Africa.

>>

Their t-shirts send out direct messages of joined-up thinking. 'No Fuel Tank' is a plea to our intelligence to cycle more; 'Children Are Born With These Arms' a reminder to us of the horrors being perpetrated in Africa. New Internationalist aims to make a difference by raising conscience and helping us "to keep an eye on our world."

'CHILDREN ARE BORN WITH THESE ARMS, NOT THESE ARMS'

Man Made°

< 9 78021 59 ORIGIN68 >

'MAN MADE: EARTH' SHIRT

"IS THERE ANYTHING WE HAVEN'T PUT A PRICE ON YET?"

Origin68 knocked around the idea of a t-shirt company "down the pub" for a few years before launching in 2007. "We were t-shirt fanatics, but we'd grown tired of the never-ending array of designs spouting the same old corporate bobbins...we yearned to express a response to our environment, surroundings and society, and hopefully to look half decent whilst we did it."

Their fresh designs are the result, kicking off with the hand-drawn 'Consume Everything' shirt. The shirt is typical of Origin68's concerns, expressing disdain for the over-commercialization and consumption which characterizes the West.

>>

'CONSUME EVERYTHING'

It reads: 'Buy lots of things, make life that little bit better, you can have it all...shit, bollocks, crap. Consume, may all your dreams come true.' Other designs include the 'Man Made: Earth' shirt, the first in a new range highlighting "man's campaign of destruction against the planet."

Origin68 have plans that will take their work beyond the canvas of the t-shirt. "At the moment we are focusing on developing and increasing our t-shirt range and getting ourselves stocked in some small independent stores. However, in the fullness of time, we hope to expand into other areas of design."

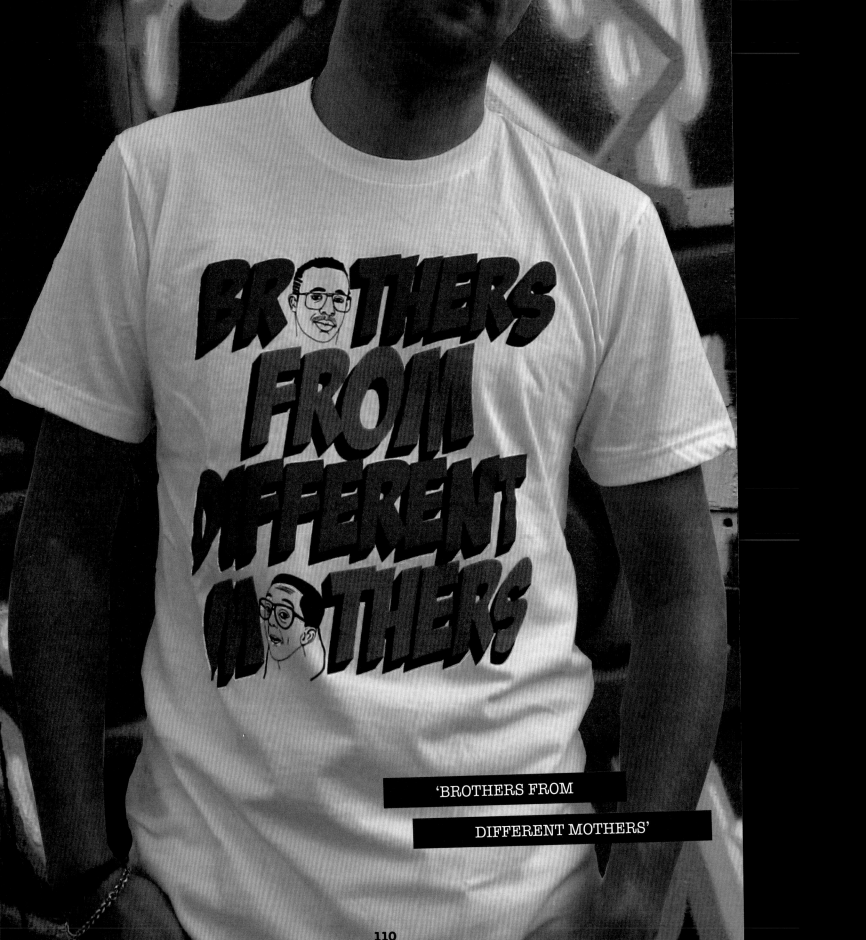

'BROTHERS FROM

DIFFERENT MOTHERS'

110

WEMOTO

'LOST SOULS FOREVER'

kisch, Patrick Lotz and Stefan Golz founded Wemoto in 2003, fulfilling the
creatively on their own brand. The trio take much of their inspiration fro
scene. They don't claim any big philosophy behind Wemoto: "Wemoto is i
a little bit more fun into the streetwear scene. People should mellow dow
everything so seriously. We're not into doing the next Louis Vuitton patt
lls's face on a t-shirt." The designs are graphically loud and the messages
, as in 'Damn Good Kids,' or 'Lost Souls Forever', featuring a Dürer engrav
of the Apocalypse.

'DAMN GOOD KIDS'

'BLIND DEAF DUMB'

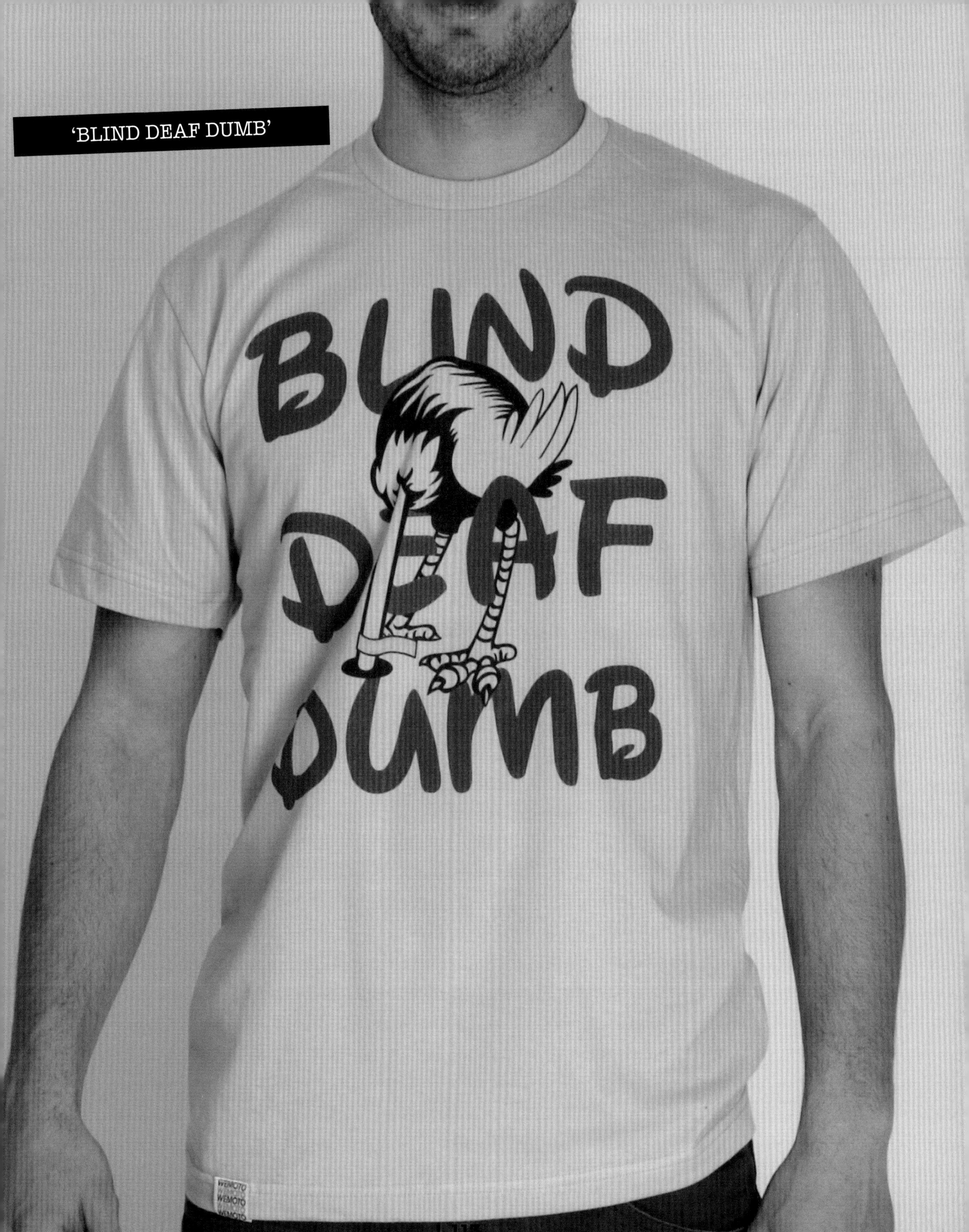

HEY! UNITE

THE ORIGINAL 'HEY! UNITE' SHIRT

THE 'COMMUNICATE' SHIRT

'AFRICA' SHIRT: SLAM DUNK POVERTY

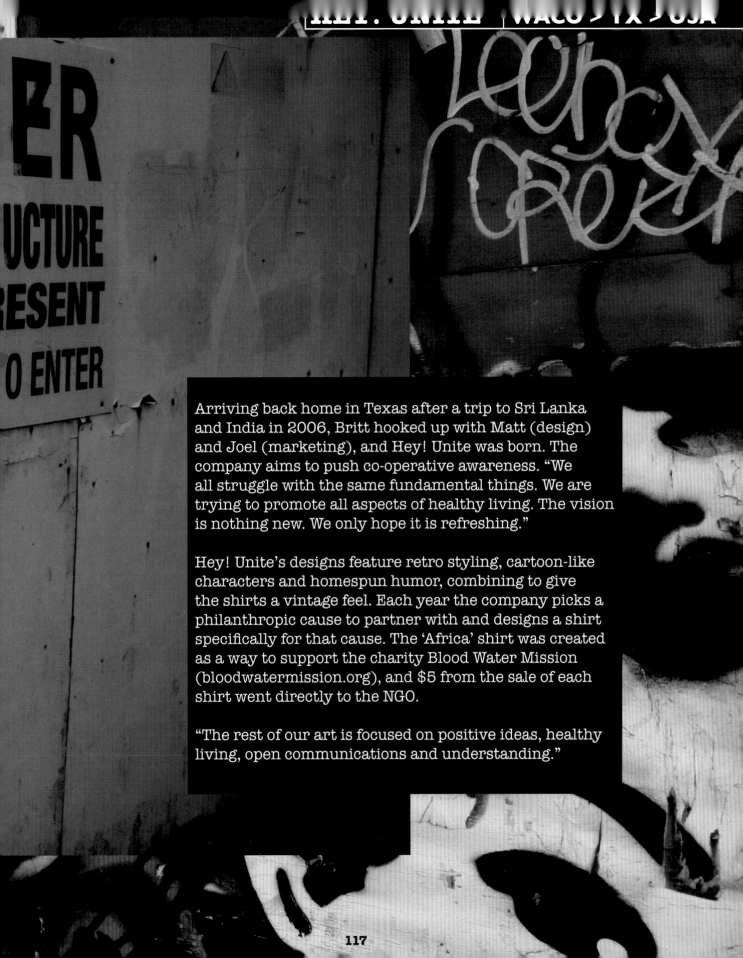

Arriving back home in Texas after a trip to Sri Lanka and India in 2006, Britt hooked up with Matt (design) and Joel (marketing), and Hey! Unite was born. The company aims to push co-operative awareness. "We all struggle with the same fundamental things. We are trying to promote all aspects of healthy living. The vision is nothing new. We only hope it is refreshing."

Hey! Unite's designs feature retro styling, cartoon-like characters and homespun humor, combining to give the shirts a vintage feel. Each year the company picks a philanthropic cause to partner with and designs a shirt specifically for that cause. The 'Africa' shirt was created as a way to support the charity Blood Water Mission (bloodwatermission.org), and $5 from the sale of each shirt went directly to the NGO.

"The rest of our art is focused on positive ideas, healthy living, open communications and understanding."

TIPPI TAPPI

'ZOOS = PRISONS'

Jenni Shortt, a passionate vegan graphic designer, created Tippi Tappi to highlight the animal and environmental causes she feels strongly about. The messages are simple and direct but Jenni says "I didn't want to point the finger at anyone or to come across as offensive."

She is strictly ethical, using organic cotton grown on independent and family-owned farms in Turkey, printing the shirts in Treviso, Italy and always using recycled and recyclable packaging. Jenni feels that "wearing a t-shirt with a slogan is an easy way to spread the word and draw the attention to the things we care about."

'I DON'T EAT ANIMALS' SHIRT: GO VEG

‘PLANT MORE TREES’

'LOVE BIRDS' SHIRT: DON'T EAT THEM

KATHARINE HAMNETT

'CHOOSE LIFE'

The most successful t-shirt designer ever, both commercially and in terms of message-impact, Katharine Hamnett sometimes expresses scepticism that buying a protest t-shirt is an excuse for inaction, a sticking plaster for a guilt trip. She for one hasn't stopped fighting since launching her first oversized protest tees in 1983: 'Choose Life' (an entreaty to practise safe sex with the advent of HIV/AIDS, but since hijacked by the pro-life lobby in the USA); 'Worldwide Nuclear Ban Now'; 'Preserve The Rainforests'; 'Save The World'; 'Save The Whales'; 'Education Not Missiles'. Brilliantly simple, big typography with a refreshing directness, they were an instant hit. Completely straightforward about what she believed, Hamnett wore her

>>

...AND KATHARINE E HAMNETT

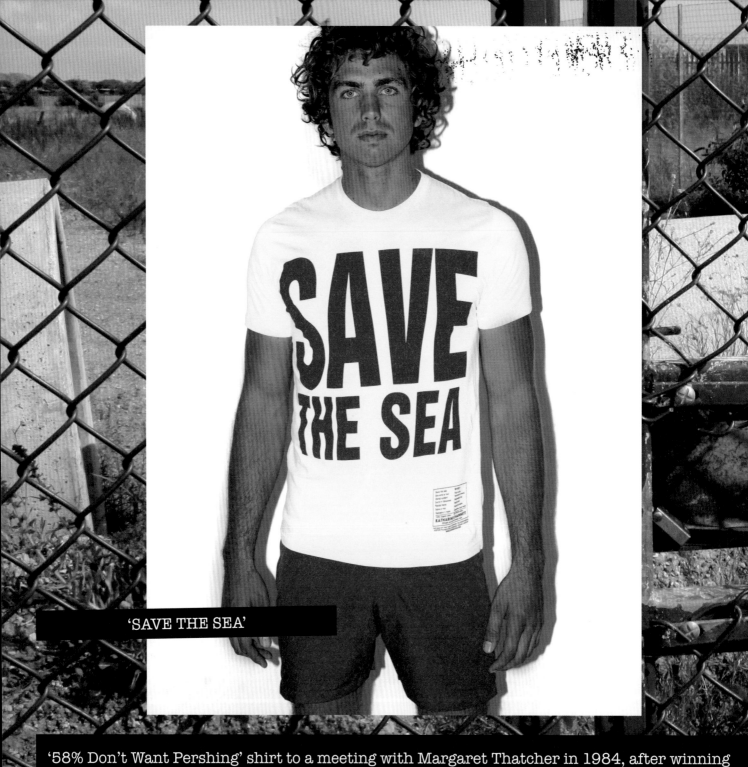

'SAVE THE SEA'

'58% Don't Want Pershing' shirt to a meeting with Margaret Thatcher in 1984, after winning Designer of the Year from the British Fashion Council. In 1987 she discovered, to her horror, that the use of pesticides by cotton producers was killing at least 10,000 people a year (now 20,000), with a further 1 million dying early from drinking water from poisoned aquifers, as a result of the impact of desertification and of longer-term pesticide poisoning. She resolved to do something about it, fighting her licensees all over the world to get them to produce ethically. She failed – they simply couldn't be bothered. One Italian manufacturer switched the fabrics for one of her collections without telling her. Hamnett was furious when she found out, but he

>>

'CLEAN UP OR DIE'

'NO MORE FASHION VICTIMS'

30

'VOTE'

'DELIVER US FROM EVIL'

Katharine, if you keep on about this ethical shit, you can take your collecti
So she did, tore up all her contracts, and started again. Change is finally co
cton is becoming the fashion industry's new standard. Now in her sixties, s
still supporting those causes she was the first to focus on 20 years ago. Th
attles to be fought: highlighting, with the Environmental Justice Foundati
crous cotton business in Uzbekistan, and her view that there is increasing
k: "the cosmetic companies don't like black models, the racist bitches, the

KINDRED

'MEET IN THE MIDDLE'

Unique and original, Kindred draw inspiration for their visual language from "the lives led by lumberjacks in the 1900s, combined with pop culture." Established in 2005, they aim as a business to "be as fair as we can, and to commit random acts of kindness."

Kindred's recent designs have highlighted unnecessary violence "on both small and large scales." They are closely involved with their community, recently founding OnRamp – a programme to help art and design students from under-funded high schools find real career opportunities, and experience, in design companies.

PRETTY HAMMER

THE 'SAVE DARFUR' SHIRT

Pretty Hammer came to life in 2005 in Sacramento, CA and now sell in retail as well as online, and in Europe as well as North America. From the start the company contributed to charitable causes – the first being the Save Darfur Organization. The aim is to help fund their chosen organizations but also "to make fashionable designs which allow people to physically support worthy causes with pride." Their production has unique touches – each shirt comes with a unique tag with a story about the shirt's subject. "We want more and more companies to feel better about earning revenue for causes greater than their own wallets" they say.

SOULD

GET THAT OIL

THE 'CRUDE REALITY' SHIRT

FROM THE F/W '08 SILENCE IS BETRAYAL COLLECTION

"The best way to describe SOULD is 'Let Your Rage Fuel Your Passion'...and we should point out that starting an independent clothing company is a TON of work; if you don't have a passion for what you're doing and why you're doing it, it will be over real quick" say founders Josh and Col. SOULD – a play on 'sold our soul' – was founded in 2005 and got into retail in 2007. They sell exclusively to boutiques and streetwear stores, and are privately held and funded, meaning they "answer to nobody." They aim to create designs that are graphically bold, yet ambiguous in theme – there is a certain love of paradox in what they do. "Our aim is not to make up your mind, but to start the conversation."

>

'NO LIMIT' SHIRT: AMERICAN EXCESS

While SOULD say that: "we can really get away with virtually anything" the lawyers of "that British 'artist' whose name rhymes with 'worst'" disagreed and demanded they destroy all examples of a t-shirt design criticizing what they perceived to be the grotesque waste and excess of the artist's diamond-encrusted skull 'For the Love of God'. SOULD say that the design of the offending shirt, called 'A Bloody Waste' (it was going to be called 'For The Love of Money') included a half-tone of the top portion of the skull, with Sierra Leone child-soldiers in the eyes.

As well as harpooning the giants of the art world, our leaders and our celebrities "(who are sadly sometimes one and the same)" SOULD say that "overall, we focus on political and social injustices and absurdities; from war-mongering presidents to girls willing to sell their bodies and anonymity for a few hundred bucks." Their range of targets also extends to the excesses of excess credit; a Western society obsessed with brands; the brainwashing provided by mainstream media; and the presence of guns in US schools, to name a few. Josh says "I want to try to spread the word to those who will listen (especially young people), that you don't have to be rich to help others."

"T-shirts, in the simplest terms, are pieces of art that allow individuals to express themselves in an instant...Luckily, we've found some people that are thinking the same way...or at least enough to keep us in business...having someone email you from across the globe and tell you they appreciate your designs...that's what it's all about." Lucky for us too, that SOULD are still in business, and as brilliantly, paradoxically and ambiguously inventive as ever.

WHO CONSUMES WHOM? THE 'BRAND FLAKES' SHIRT

"FORTIFIED WITH ZERO COMMON SENSE"

THE 'TERRORDOME' SHIRT

FEATURING THE US SENATE

THE 'DADDY'S LITTLE GIRLS' SHIRT: DRAFT THE BOURGEOISIE

HIGH SOCIETY GIRLS WEAR BALL GOWNS ACCESSORIZED WITH AK-47S

THE 'CHOICE IS YOURS' SHIRT

FROM THE SILENCE IS BETRAYAL COLLECTION

WE ARE ALL WITNESSES.

THE 'HARD TRUTH' SHIRT

WE ARE ALL WITNESSES

OPEN WIDE: 'GREED SWALLOWS'

I GOT MORE
GLOCKS & TECHS
THAN YOU

Don't forget your lunch

THE 'PACKED FOR SCHOOL' SHIRT

THE 'EMPTY' SHIRT

THE 'SLIE AS A FOX' SHIRT

THE 'MOMMY'S DROWNING' SHIRT

NOT JUST TABLOID FODDER: BRITNEY IS A MOTHER, LEST WE FORGET

73,955 FRIENDS ⚜ ZERO DIGNITY

THE '73,955 FRIENDS' SHIRT: BACK VIEW

THE '73,955 FRIENDS' SHIRT

PROJET M

THE 'ANARCHIC' SHIRT

Projet M describe themselves as "urban, ethical and chic." Manufacturing only in their native France means that they can keep a close watch on their suppliers' working conditions. Staying true to the mantra of the French Revolution – Liberté, Egalité, Fraternité – is important to founder Antoine Seve. "We are for human beings and against capitalism...I want a better world for our children; I love children from New York the same as children from Baghdad," he says. The designs are direct, as in the hand-written addition of "& Bagdad" (note French spelling) to an I Love NY t-shirt – gently emphasizing how easy it is to forget the non-Western, unmarketed and unbranded majority of humanity.

'I LOVE NY AND BAGDAD'

JE SUIS
LA MORT

HANS AND FRAS

'DEATHMASK' SHIRT

Hans and Fras have a simple company philosophy, "Have Fun", and are suitably self-deprecating about their principles: "We stand for truth, justice, freedom and mandarin oranges. Straight from the can, man. Love those things." More seriously, they are passionate about a whole load of causes: AIDS research, access to medication for poor countries, a real solution for Iraq that puts people first and oil last, to name a few. They consciously seek visual inspiration from all over the world: "it's easy to become blinded to the world outside the US when you live here," and still print all of their shirts by hand, so that each one is slightly different and unique, "like the person buying it."

HIPPYTREE

THE HIPPYTREE 'PEACE' SHIRT

HippyTree grew out of founder Andrew Sarnecki's experiments in urban art in the South Bay area of L.A.. He started selling t-shirts out of his bedroom in Hermosa Beach in 2003 and now "my friend Josh runs the sales end." They don't have a written set of company principles, but talk "about our ideals all the time." HippyTree keep their products away from events and shops that don't mesh with their interests. "We stay away from things like politics and mass commercialism...and try to intertwine our passion for surfing with our interests in nature."

Many of HippyTree's designs reference their love of surfing, nature and sustainable living. A recent collection was inspired by Boy Scout uniforms and merit badges, the latter being transformed into pro-nature messages.

THE 'NATURE IS COMING' SHIRT

JOHN YATES
AT ALTERNATIVE TENTACLES

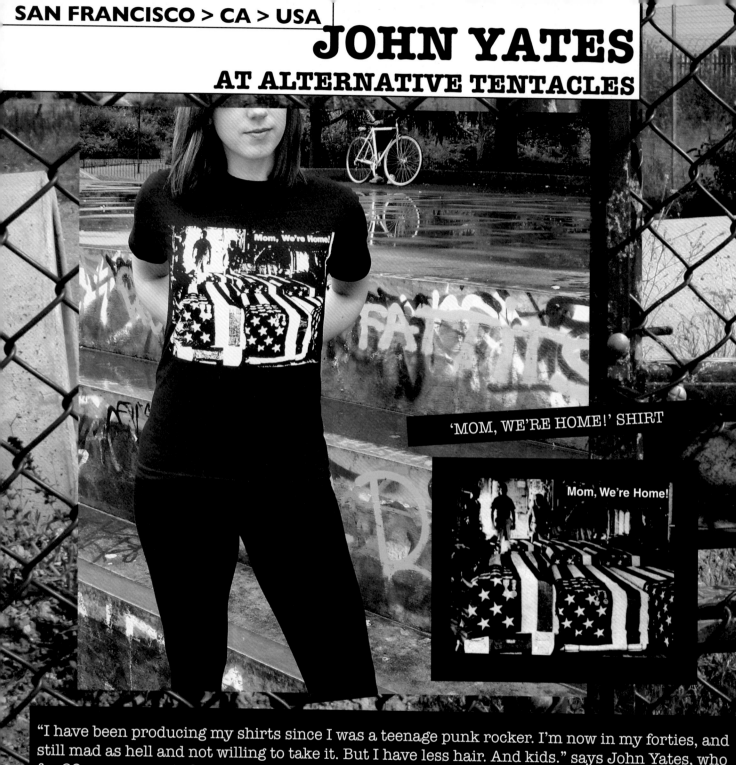

'MOM, WE'RE HOME!' SHIRT

"I have been producing my shirts since I was a teenage punk rocker. I'm now in my forties, and still mad as hell and not willing to take it. But I have less hair. And kids." says John Yates, who for 20 years operated under the moniker Stealworks. John still celebrates "being just me. I don't have to worry about offending or upsetting anyone, because, let's be honest, no one cares what I do. I'm just shooting my mouth off via t-shirts. Preaching to the converted. Because someone has to."

This irreverence and directness has seen John's designs sold by a number of companies, including Alternative Tentacles. Founded by Jello Biafra, AT are primarily a music label, have been around since 1979, and provide a great outlet for artists who work outside the corporate music industry – "we chose the bands and people to work with based on their creativity and their ethics." They are big on human rights, environmental and anti-war causes.

In answer to our question, what causes do you support? John told us: "Whataya got? There's a lot out there, but essentially I support the human cause. And that's not as preachy as it probably comes across. I basically try to treat people I meet in life in a manner I would want to be treated. It's a simple approach, but acting decently toward one another doesn't have to be rocket science. I'm left-leaning, obviously, but I like to think for myself. I don't subscribe to any particular system or party or group. I can't afford the rates."

'DEMOCRACY: WE DELIVER'

'AMERICA: BUSINESS AS USUAL'

BACK OF SHIRT READS: WILL MORE LIVES LOST REALLY MAKE YOU SAFER?

JOHN YATES
FOR MIGHTY HEALTHY

OFFICER

FRIENDLY?

'OFFICER FRIENDLY?' SHIRT

WE SWIM AGAINST THE TIDE

WITHIN YOUR MAINSTREAM

'WE SWIM AGAINST THE TIDE WITHIN YOUR MAINSTREAM'

N.Y.C.'s Mighty Healthy try to operate according to the implications of their company name. "That phrase serves as a goal for all of us, regardless of age, background or location." They pick designs and designers that are "aesthetically pleasing, clever, identifiable by a wide range of people, but not necessarily the mainstream consumer."

John Yates's designs for them for Fall '08 have the raw energy, dark humor and verbal wit of the best of punk and new wave – there are echoes of The Clash here. They meet Yates's own criteria of creating t-shirts that are "bold, confrontational and, ideally, intelligent."

'LIFE'S A RIOT, GET OUT MORE'

SOY

'MAKE BEATS NOT WAR'

"Revolution means change, making wrong into right, and building awareness for a higher consciousness. SOY is the army of people that live to fight for these things. Stand. Overcome. Yell!" say SOY (from the Spanish 'I am'). SOY, founded in Seattle in 2001, have chosen to do this through their t-shirt designs. They describe themselves as "a streetwear company that offers quality clothing with design substance."

SOY's messages are direct, but the visual language always has a subtext. "We are inspired by the past, the present, and the future, with an underlying emphasis on all things revolutionary. We also turn to worldwide cultures and subcultures for inspiration. Life overall inspires us!"

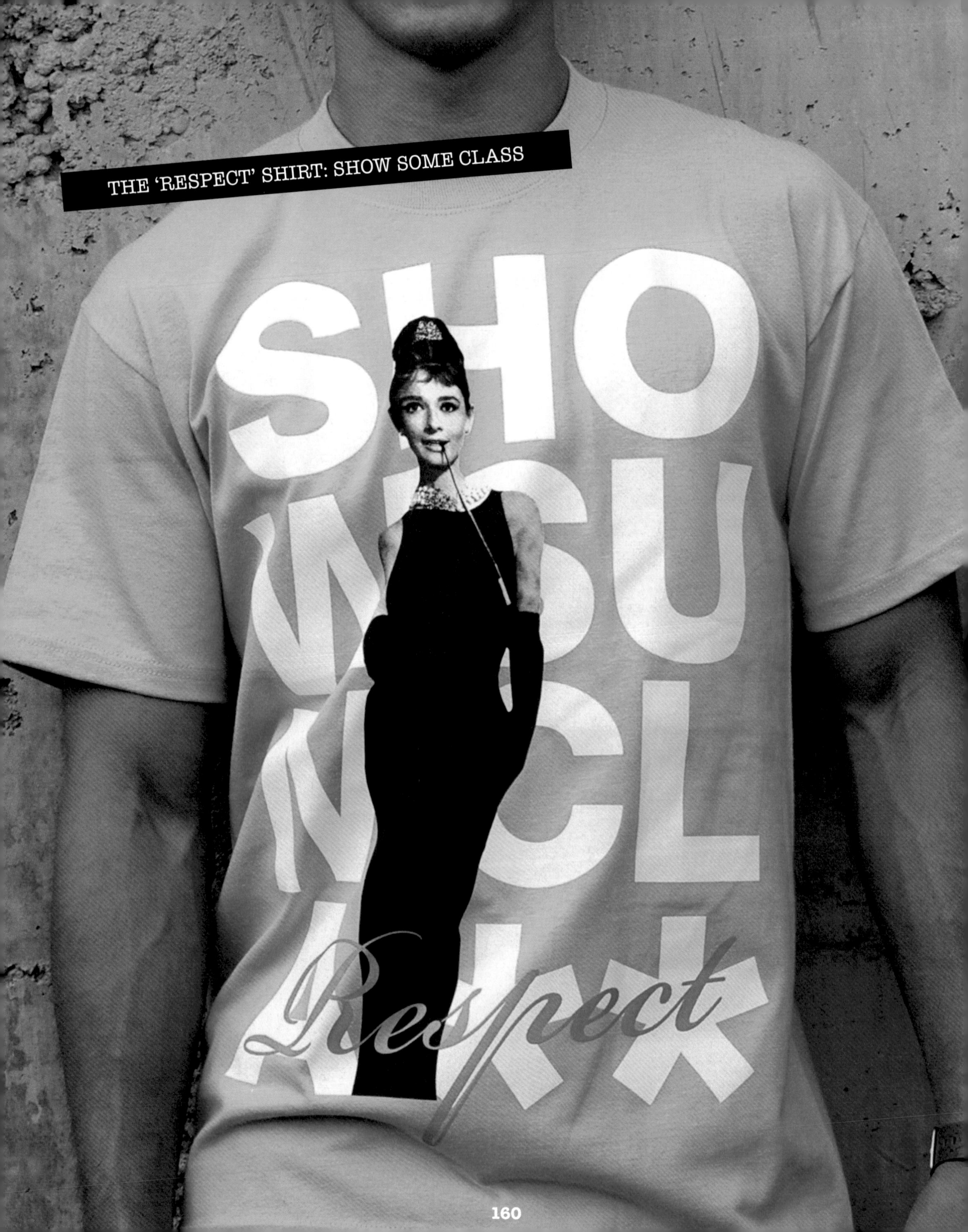

THE 'RESPECT' SHIRT: SHOW SOME CLASS

'FREEDOM ISN'T FREE'

THE 'WELCOME TO AMERICA' SHIRT

WELCOME
TO
AMERICA

PINK FLOYD-STYLE TYPOGRAPHY

LEAVE
US
KIDS

ALONE

'CHOOSE YOUR WEAPON'

THE PEN AND THE SWORD

SMASH YOUR TV:

'THINK OUTSIDE THE BOX'

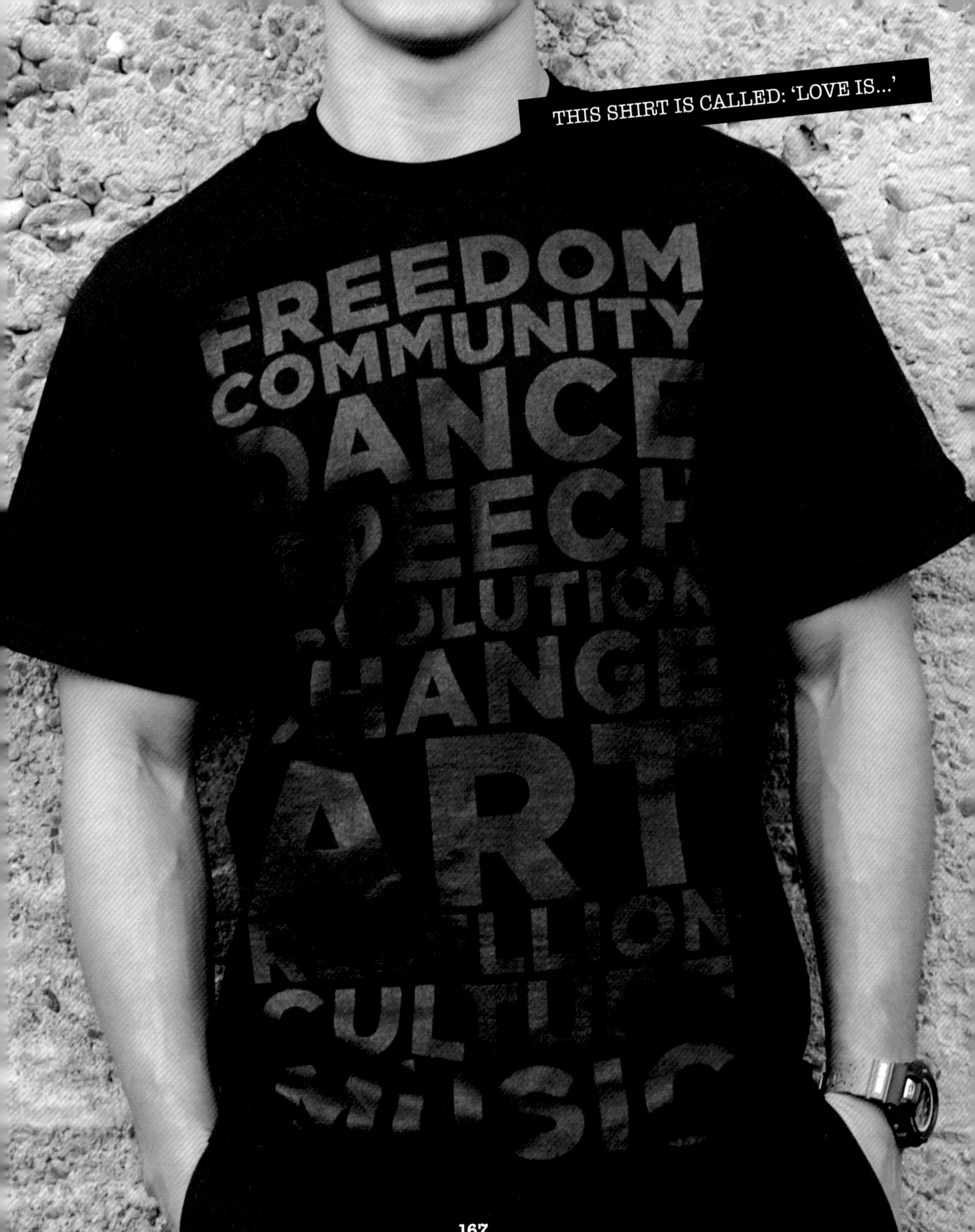
FREEDOM
COMMUNITY
ART

THIS SHIRT IS CALLED: 'LOVE IS...'

WRONGWROKS

'UNIVRESITY OF FLAWS'

"Making art these days is no longer about details, clearness, perfection...coz digital kills... everyone is a photographer, fuck, it's not fun anymore" says Tony Wong, the designer behind Wrongwroks (wrong works/wrong rocks). Wong hit upon the mistake vein at art school, after learning screen printing, and launched his online store out of Vancouver in 2005. By 2006 the brand was becoming a real success – the 'Kate Moss' shirt sold out within two hours of being released in Takashima City, Japan.

Wong's designs are available in stores in Europe and South-East Asia. He is "big in Japan" but not as bothered about conquering North America. In an interview with ION mag he said: "When people first see my stuff they think it's kind of fake and I'm ripping off someone. Like the **>>**

'UPREME: MONA LISA RIPPED OFF' TEE

THE 'THOUSAND WORDS' SHIRT

'WCDONALD BLACK ON BLACK' SHIRT

'WCDONALD GOLD ON BLACK' SHIRT

THE 'KATE MOSS AMERICAN IDOL' SHIRT

Supreme logo or Doraemon. Japanese are really strict about counterfeits and it doesn't exist in that culture. Later, when they pick up what it is though, boom, everyone wants it."

Wong borrows visual icons from the disparate worlds of cartoons, celebrity, art and corporate branding and remixes them in a hierarchy-free mish mash. The corporates can't have it both ways, he seems to be saying: you try and become part of the language, you open yourself up to being shaken up. But they seem to love it: "They'll use the same graphic and collaborate with a real company and make a whole bunch of clothes. With Doraemon they did the same thing as me except with no Adidas sneakers." So what would he make of being imitated? The copyright notice on his website tells anyone thinking of ripping him off: All Wrongs Reserved.

THE 'RIPPED OFF' SHIRT

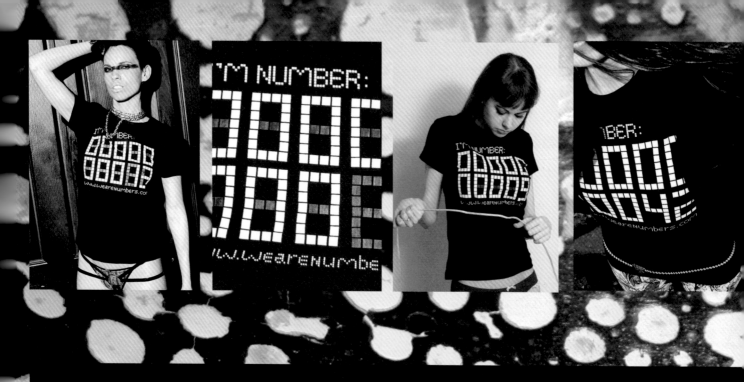

We Are Numbers make a point of celebrating everyone's uniqueness by reducing everyone to a number. The company started as a conceptual art project and the whole thing somehow works, because the t-shirts are at once the same (the numbers constructed from a digital matrix) and yet every number is unique. You look at the individual, not the message, or the design, or the attempt to influence through fashion signifiers linked to invidious marketing.

Their website says: "We are equal. We are different. We are individuals. We are a group. We are fashion cynics, because we are beautiful as we are. We are living and loving today." We Are Numbers start with a t-shirt printed with ten number eights; once you have ordered a shirt, you take the next available number and they black out the relevant squares to make your shirt. Witty, quirky and wonderfully unlikely from one of the most fashion-conscious cities in Europe.

NUMBER 15

GOATBOY

'WHO WOULD JESUS BOMB?'

Who would Jesus bomb?

Goat Boy was set up by Adam Hunt and Peter Le Gras in 2008 in Pyrmont, Australia. "In a world gone mad, irony will set you free" is their company philosophy, as the sales pitch for their 'Peace' shirt demonstrates: "Guns suck but fuck they look cool. So to give you an excuse to pack some heat on your chest, we've got all bent up over a couple of legendary AK-47s. Peace." Goatboy are extremely precise about where they source their t-shirts: "we use sweat-shop free American Apparel," and about their manufacturing process: "traditional silk-screen printing because digital printing sucks." Other than that, they have, refreshingly, "a distinct lack of principles."

>>

THE 'PEACE' SHIRT

THE PEACE SIGN IS MADE OF GUNS AND AMMO

'OSAMAS IN PYJAMAS'

THE 'LIBERTY' SHIRT

On the subject of corporate logos Goatboy are strident: "we don't do logos. Corporations spend millions convincing billions that it's cool to wear their logo. It's not cool. Wearing a t-shirt with a logo on it is a bizarre form of corporate fellatio. It's prostitution – you pay them to fuck you with their brand. Goatboy doesn't understand why people wear logos on their bodies like a temporary tattoo."

Ironic and blunt in classic Ozzie fashion, though they admit: "we'd probably change our minds about that if a national clothing chain threw enough money at us."

THE 'PEACE' SHIRT

ADAM HUNT
FOR AMNESTY

'WEAPONS OF MASS DESTRUCTION'

Before creating Goatboy, Adam Hunt was one of Australia's leading creatives, as Creative Director of Sydney agency, Belgiovane Williams Mackay; some of his work whilst at BWM made it into the permanent collection at MoMA, N.Y.C.. It was the amazing success of his designs for Amnesty that persuaded him to go it alone – "'Kerching' rang loud through my beer-addled brain." The 'Mosquito' shirt for Amnesty has been re-issued many times. In addition to Goatboy, Adam has published *Pregnancy – A Man's Survival Guide*, and also runs a "boutique shit-stirring agency, AKTIVIST, which will be out there generating noise."

TOWEL-HEAD.
QUEUE
JUMPER.
ILLEGAL
IMMIGRANT.

THE 'HUMAN' SHIRT

"If you think you are too small
to make a difference -
try sleeping with a mosquito"
- Dalai Lama

A DALAI LAMA QUOTE: "IF YOU THINK YOU ARE TOO SMALL

TO MAKE A DIFFERENCE – TRY SLEEPING WITH

A MOSQUITO"

"Those who can make
you believe absurdities
can make you
commit atrocities."

- Voltaire

A QUOTE FROM VOLTAIRE:

"THOSE WHO CAN MAKE YOU BELIEVE ABSURDITIES

CAN MAKE YOU COMMIT ATROCITIES"

ARE YOU GENERIC?

censorship causes blindness

Some of the smartest cultural jammers around, Are You Generic?, founded by insomniac artist Okat, have been set up since 2001. They've become known for their anti-print media campaign (distributing leaflets to insert into glossy magazines at newsagents, pointing out that most editorial is just advertorial) and their anti-Starbucks critique, plastering hoardings for a new Starbucks in Miami (they had a point – there were seven within one city block) with the paste-up "I love a good Starbucks Invasion."

Are You Generic? are a group of artists that seek to question, protest and disprove. "Our nemeses are unethical corporations, censorship, the slanted media, hypocrisy, excessive advertising, and plain stupidity."

>>

THE 'MONKEY' SHIRT

YOU BOMB ME, I BOMB YOU

MONKEY SEE, MONKEY DO

THE 'RESIST MUCH' T-SHIRT

'DOMESTIC ESPIONAGE'

'GIVE BRAND AMERICA THE FINGER'

'TRASH YOUR TELEVISION'

Are You Generic? also see their catalog of t-shirt designs and print as an exhibition of street art intended to critique and reclaim "social and mental environments." They are massively anti-brand: "our shirts promote a concept, NOT a name (not even our own); the shirts have no label, no brand, no logo, and are printed on sweatshop-free tees."

The designs are calls to action, from 'Give Brand America The Finger' to their popular 'Resist Much, Obey Little'. The pervasive power of the media, and in particular broadcast corporations, are targets, but the attacks never lose their edge of humor.

FAT AMERICAN

'TERRORISM' SHIRT DETAIL: THE TWIN TOWERS IN THE DISTANCE

Asked by his brother to help run a screen printing business, Alex Boeckl left his dead-end art studio job in Orange County, FL, and started printing t-shirts. When a clerk with a heavy French accent screamed at a skinny guy in his neighborhood store "You fat American pig! Get the fuck out of my shoppe!" a brand was born.

The first shirt showed a fat guy in a reclining chair, wearing only underpants, clenching a clicker and smiling apathetically. Then 9/11 happened and Fat American changed its focus to critique the Bush administration's misdirected revenge attack on Iraq. Fat American took an active part in the anti-war movement, demonstrating in New York, D.C. and Ft. Benning, GA. By 2003, the company was sponsoring local university students to attend the next few D.C. protests, "but the slow-down in the movement left me disillusioned by the whole experience."

THE 'TERRORISM' SHIRT

'AMERICAN EMPIRE' SHIRT AND DETAIL

THE 'BOOK POWER' SHIRT

'WATA DISMAL WORLD' SHIRT

'WATA DISMAL WORLD' DETAIL

Fat American's t-shirts critique right-wing foreign policy adventures and the lack of care of recent administrations for the disadvantaged. They have worked closely with photographer Wheat Wurtzburger, including on the shoot featured here. A previous collaboration saw homeless men and women model Fat American t-shirts.

Boeckl supports local causes – "I recently launched a project on my website whereby I work with a group or organization to print and sell their t-shirt and send them all of the profits" – but feels that it is hard to say whether he is influencing any positive change. "I'd say we aren't making things worse. I could just as easily have become a soldier or an engineer for a weapons manufacturer."

YOU MAY RECOGNIZE THE TYPOGRAPHY ON THIS SHIRT...

'SWEAT SHOP': ALWAYS LOW STANDARDS

THE 'MONSTER TRUCKS' SHIRT

KOWTOW

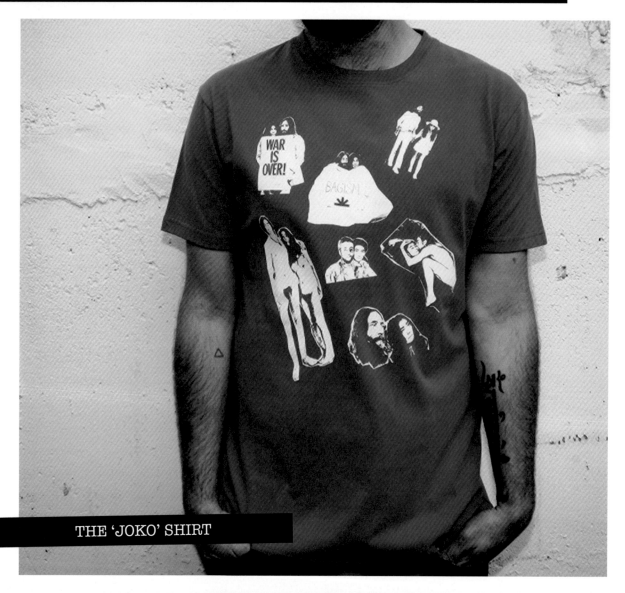

THE 'JOKO' SHIRT

Kowtow launched their first collection in 2007. 100% certified Fair Trade and Organic, they give 2% of their net invoice value to the Fairtrade Labelling Organisation. They aim "to inspire and to be thought-provoking with a global perspective" and their designs are about "politics, tongue-in-cheek humor, ethics, nature fighting back, anti-commercialism, freedom fighting, anti-war, equality, music (they support local bands by giving away compilation CDs with each garment), and anything else that tickles our fancy."

Many of Kowtow's designs highlight the Iraq War. 'Joko' makes the point that no one in the music business has been as effectively anti-war as John and Yoko in the 60s; 'War is Over', from the Lennon song, suggests that it could be, if the US government wanted it that way.

>>

'WAR IS OVER' SHIRT

'GUNS DON'T KILL PEOPLE, POLITICIANS DO'

'Guns Don't Kill People, Politicians Do' was inspired by the neo-con cabal directing the Iraq War, with its estimated 600,000 civilian casualties. They are particularly scathing about Dick Cheney, his association with Halliburton and the contracts his ex-company have won in Iraq in the post-war 'reconstruction'.

They also focus designs on other causes. 'Matador' points out that bull-fighting is not entirely devoid of beauty: "there is nothing more beautiful than seeing a bullfighter impaled by a bull's horn." 'Skinny, White, Rich' shows how the anorexic bodies peddled by fashion magazines are sold as an aspiration for women who have it all.

>>

'MATADOR' SHIRT

The other main thread in Kowtow's thinking is the environment. The image of a Hummer "being arse-raped by a horny rhino" is payback for everything a Hummer represents in their eyes: the epitome of egotistical capitalism, and the obscenity of US soldiers risking their lives patrolling the oilfields in Iraq, so that the boys back home can fill up their civilian tanks. Our willingness to put up with pollution, even though it harms both nature and our children's health, is illustrated by 'Alice', showing Lewis Carroll's heroine wearing a gasmask.

But nature will fight back, say Kowtow: "that's the meaning of the 'Yak' shirt. The yak, looking timeless, is crushing the decaying technology of the car." Continuing this theme, Kowtow's future projects include a collaboration with the World Wildlife Fund (WWF).

'HUMMER' SHIRT: "THE MACHINE IS BEING

ARSE-RAPED BY A HORNY RHINO"

'WHITE, SKINNY, RICH'

'YAK' SHIRT: NATURE FIGHTS BACK

'ALICE' SHIRT

LEWIS CARROLL'S HEROINE WEARING A GAS MASK

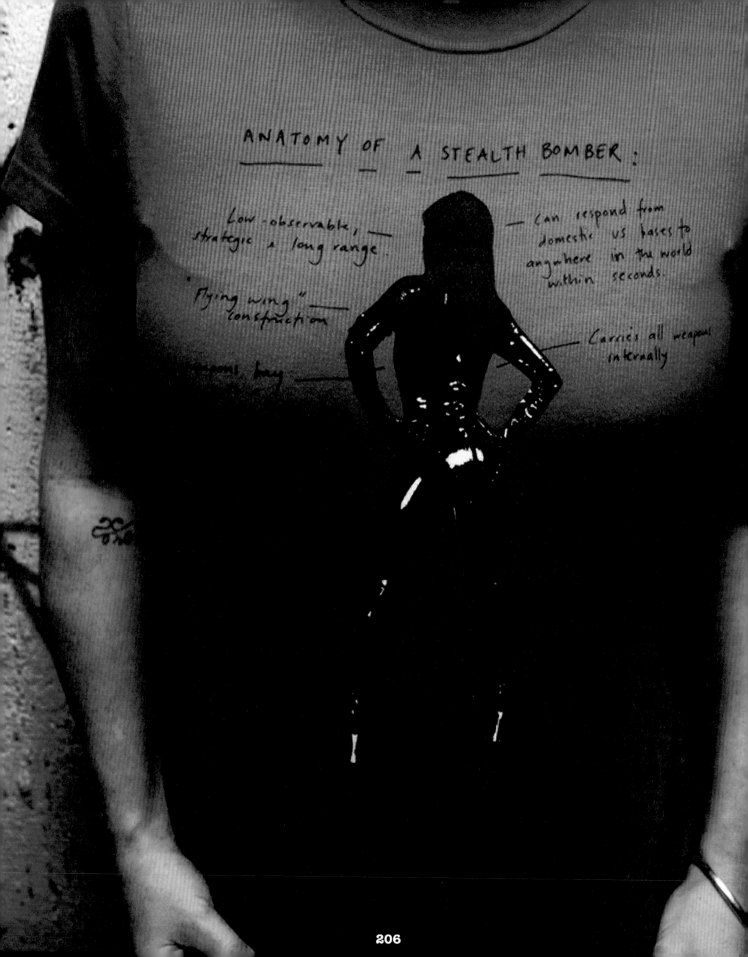

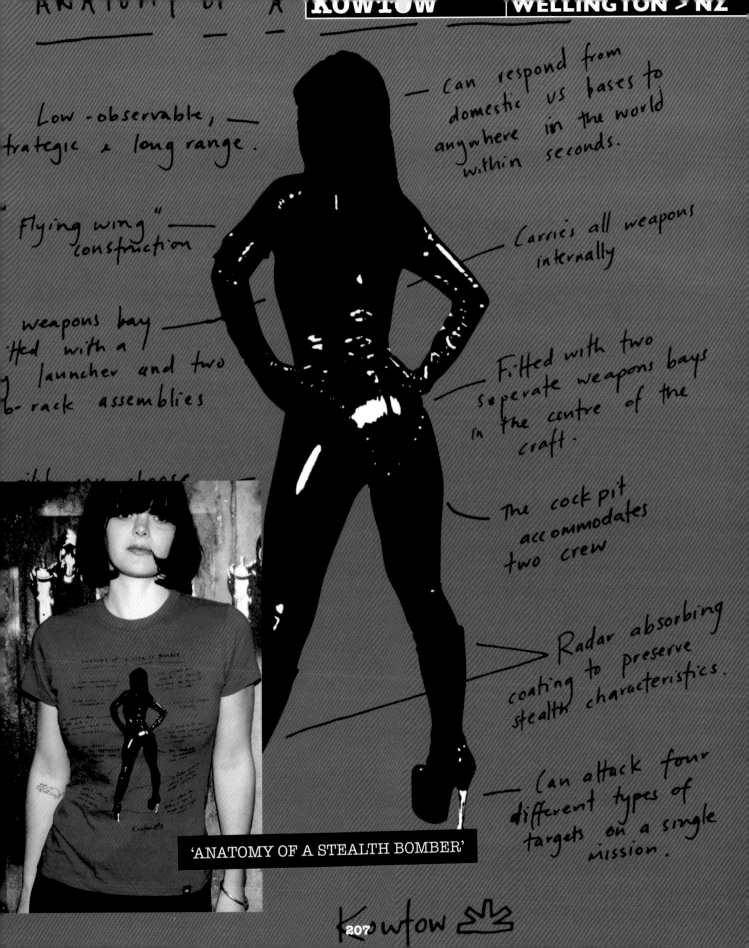

Low -observable, — trategic & long range.

— Can respond from domestic US bases to anywhere in the world within seconds.

"Flying wing" — construction

Carries all weapons internally

weapons bay ftted with a launcher and two b-rack assemblies

Fitted with two seperate weapons bays in the centre of the craft.

The cock pit accommodates two crew

Radar absorbing coating to preserve stealth characteristics.

Can attack four different types of targets on a single mission.

'ANATOMY OF A STEALTH BOMBER'

THE 'HOME GROWN' SHIRT

ILK INDUSTRIES

THE 'I LIKE TREES' SHIRT

Launched in 2004 in Edinburgh, Scotland, ILK are big on their ethical credentials: "We'd rather sell 100 t-shirts that were made ethically than 1000 that were made in a sweatshop." They focus on trying to highlight the wonders of nature over fast-paced, no-time, consumption-obsessed city living. Their first t-shirt said "Look Outside," with a picture of a camper van "as we like the idea of not settling for the status quo, pushing yourself to keep thinking, and refocusing..." Their messages are direct and each design is limited edition; when they run out of stock, they generate a new design. The latest collection is inspired by "wholesome, creative living" – simple things like making music, growing vegetables, and appreciating the beauty of what's outside our front doors.

R-EV

REPÚBLICA DE CHIGÜIRIN

'REPUBLICA DE CHIGUIRIN' BY AKITOY

THE DESIGN MIMICS THE FLAG OF THE CALIFORNIA REPUBLIC

THE CAPYBARA, A SYMBOL FOR LAZYNESS IN VENEZUELA, APPEARS INSTEAD OF A BEAR

Southern California-based r-ev.net is a Latin American graphic design network, set up to support Hispanic underground creative culture. "We're not a clothing company; we're here to add a little something to the battle against corporate giants, unbalanced consumerism, cultural pollution and the abuse of natural resources." The company target their shirts at the minorities that they represent: "we keep it low-key and underground. Our symbols, images, codes and messages are not easily understood by the common consumer."

>>

REPÚBLICA DEL CHIGÜIRÍN

THE DESIGN SUGGESTS THAT VENEZUELA IS MIMICKING THE EARLY DAYS OF THE CALIFORNIA REPUBLIC IN UNDERGOING HUGO CHAVEZ'S "BOLIVARIAN REVOLUTION"

'EL CHECK' SHIRT – CHE IN BLING

R-ev's t-shirts contain provocative comments on Latin American politics. The great hero, Che Guevara, is protrayed as a bling-wearing gangster; Venezuela's Hugo Chavez is sent up as the leader of a lazy, lawless, corrupt republic run on the early Californian Republic model. "We want to point out the duality between capitalism and communism; between consumerism and religion." R-ev.net's core design influences are still rooted in American visual culture however: skateboarding and video games are particular sources of inspiration.

KONGA®

evolucion

DETAIL OF 'EL CHECK' SHIRT

LANZY

'ANTIWAR SKULL' DETAIL

Lanzy Clothing Co was launched by boyfriend and girlfriend Guojeck Loo and Esther Liang in Ipoh, Malaysia in 2008. "Love and peace are our main concerns" they declare. "We just want to do the right thing in our own way. We are not here to compete against other companies or brands. We want to be original and true to ourselves. We just design about the things that strike us in daily life; the messages we think should be spread to max peace and love. They may be small gestures, but little changes can make a big difference." Lanzy's designs reflect these concerns: they are anti-war and anti-child labour. The t-shirts are all produced with care and in limited-edition runs.

'ANTIWAR SKULL' SHIRT

'FAKE KILLS!' SHIRT

'FAKE KILLS!' DETAIL

TURTLEHEAD

Based in Dublin, Ireland, Turtlehead are an art and fashion collective who produce designs which are "either subversive, or just stuff which tickles our funny bones." Keith Walsh founded the company, and kicked off with six of his own designs. Since then, Chris Judge, Will St. Ledger and David Shrigley have all contributed work. Over 14 designers from around the world are now designing t-shirts for the company. "We take submissions from anyone we think is good. If we like it, we fund it and share profits."

>>

One of their first shirts was 'Gay Whales for Nuclear Disarmament' – covering as many issues as possible in one go. The designs here, a collaboration with The Polyphonic Spree, all use the loveheart, the sign of love, to make symbols of war. Turtlehead list a series of charities on their website and update the list regularly. Web visitors can vote on this poll and the charity with the highest percentage of votes every three months is awarded 5% of the company's profits.

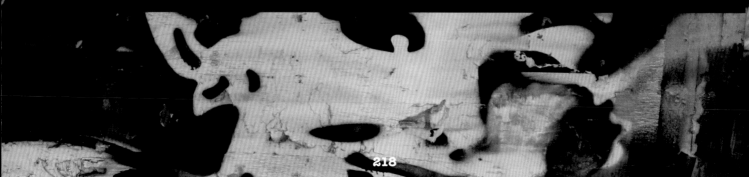

'LOVE GRENADE' SHIRT

THE 'LOVE TANK' SHIRT

THE 'LOVE PLANE' SHIRT

TOO BLACK GUYS

Adrian Aitcheson launched Too Black Guys in Canada in 1990. The company was well known as a hip-hop brand throughout the 90s, with a flagship shop in N.Y.C. until 1999. Aitcheson subsequently worked for Canadian brand Roots, and, as special project clothing designer for the company, he designed the Canadian and U.S. team gear for the 2002 Winter Olympics. In 2006 he decided to relaunch Too Black Guys.

For a streetwear brand, Too Black Guys stands out because of its willingness to tackle the subject of race head on. The company wants to make fashion worthwhile and relevant: "our company philosophy is to add purpose to product in a way that does not compromise the highest level of quality or design." The shirts shown here do this by highlighting the racial history and civil rights movement of the U.S.. They are from the 'House of Crow' collection, which references the Jim Crow Laws enacted in 1876 in many U.S. states. The laws resulted in the de facto segregation of blacks and whites in public schools, public transportation, restrooms and restaurants, and were not properly repealed until 1964.

>>

It takes talent to turn what could seem like a history lesson into accessible, and even desirable, fashion. As the logo for the collection – a grinning cartoon crow – shows, Too Black Guys treat the subject with a light touch, using humor to insert the past into contemporary popular culture. They can steer pretty close to the edge, as in the 'Slavery Sucked!' shirt, featuring a Peanuts-style cartoon of a redneck baby screaming. Aitcheson explains their intentions: "our company principle is to approach the subject matter of our themes with cultural sensitivity and critical honesty. We do not aim to exploit, or sensationalize and we will not make anything that we would not feel comfortable wearing ourselves."

Too Black Guys designs promise to remain refreshingly direct. When asked what subjects he will tackle, Aitcheson says: "anything that we think is relevant and that we have a clear perspective on."

'JIM CROW COUTURE'

FROM THE HOUSE OF CROW COLLECTION

'SLAVERY SUCKED!' DETAIL

'SLAVERY SUCKED!' S

FROM THE HOUSE OF CROW COLLECTIO

HOUSE of CROW

SOME OF MY BEST FRIENDS ARE BLACK

'SOME OF MY BEST FRIENDS ARE BLACK'

SOME OF MY
BEST FRIENDS ARE
WHITE

'SOME OF MY BEST FRIENDS ARE WHITE'

'EMMETT TILL' SHIRT

BLACK YOUTH EMMETT TILL WAS 14 WHEN

HE WENT TO STAY WITH HIS UNCLE IN MISSISSIPPI, IN SUMMER 1955.

HE WAS MURDERED BY WHITE LOCALS AFTER WOLF-WHISTLING AT WHITE GROCERY STORE-

VNER, CAROLYN BRYANT. HIS EYE WAS GOUGED OUT AND HIS BODY THROWN IN THE RIVER .

TILL'S MOTHER INSISTED ON AN OPEN CASKET FOR THE FUNERAL IN CHICAGO

SO THE WORLD COULD SEE THE BRUTALITY OF HIS KILLING.

THE EVENT WAS A DEFINING MOTIVATOR FOR THE U.S. CIVIL RIGHTS MOVEMENT

THE RADICAL REPUBLICANS WHO EMERGED IN

1854 OPPOSED LINCOLN'S TERMS FOR ENDING THE CIVIL WAR AND WANTED A QUICKER

END TO SLAVERY AND HARSHER

CONSEQUENCES FOR THE CONFEDERATE STATES WHO TRIED TO SECEDE.

AFTER THE WAR THEY FOUGHT FOR THE CIVIL RIGHTS OF FREEDMEN AND HELPED

REBUILD THE SOUTH – VERY DIFFERENT TO THE

OUT OF TOUCH IMAGE THE PARTY HAS TODAY

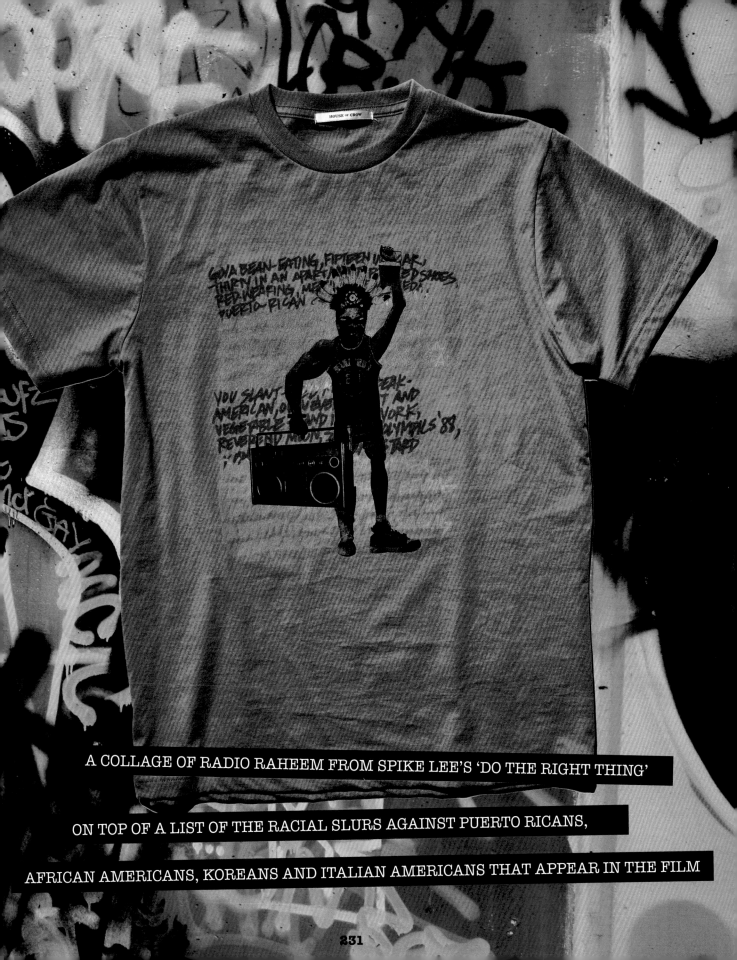

A COLLAGE OF RADIO RAHEEM FROM SPIKE LEE'S 'DO THE RIGHT THING'

ON TOP OF A LIST OF THE RACIAL SLURS AGAINST PUERTO RICANS,

AFRICAN AMERICANS, KOREANS AND ITALIAN AMERICANS THAT APPEAR IN THE FILM

'LIBERATE U.S.': THE U.S. GOVERNMENT SAID IT INVADED IRAQ

TO DELIVER 'FREEDOM', YET HAS DECIMATED FREEDOMS AT HOME

KLAUS INDUSTRIES

'MEET LINCOLN': THE FIRST REPUBLICAN PRESIDENT WOULD

HAVE A LOT TO TEACH GEORGE BUSH

"When I started Klaus Industries I didn't intend for the designs to be rooted in politics" says founder Grant Davis. "My original intention was to simply make shirts that I would want to wear, because at the time most t-shirts were over-designed in an attempt to be super chic, or just an advertisement for a brand, or a lame one-line joke." Davis found inspiration elsewhere: " I started making shirts in 2005. At the time the majority of people in the U.S. were still in favor of the war in Iraq. Bush and his gang were shredding civil rights and lying about everything. Most people were just blindly following along. It was crazy.

>>

DETAIL OF GOVERNOR OF CALIFORNIA ARNOLD SCHWARZENEGGER

The media was regurgitating everything they said and people believed it and everything seemed hopeless. Soon everything I was designing seemed to be political, so I just gave into that early on." A range of issues are highlighted by Davis, from the lack of proper political scrutiny of the Bush administration – "he behaves like a monarch" – to the rise of surveillance by the State.

He also pokes fun at the hypocrisy of anti-immigration Republicans who tried to get the constitution altered so Arnie could run for President, pointing out the color-bias of the move. The brand also looks backwards – its 'Lincoln' shirt highlights how divorced the Bush administration has been from the principles of the first Republican President.

'IMMIGRANT' SHIRT: "A LOT OF THE PEOPLE WHO ARE 'ANTI-IMMIGRANT'

DON'T NECESSARILY HAVE THOSE FEELINGS IF THE IMMIGRANT IN QUESTION

ISN'T POOR AND BROWN SKINNED"

SURVEILLANCE STATE:
'TWO THOUSAND AND EIGHT
IS THE NEW 1984'

'GOD SURVEY THE KING' DETAIL

'GOD SURVEY THE KING' SHIRT

THE GRETEST

'KILL MONDAYS' SHIRT

Madrid-based The Gretest was founded by Grete in 2008. She says that she "doesn't support any causes right now," but instead concentrates on making t-shirts with a rebellious message that are "completely individual." All of the shirts produced by The Gretest are hand-printed and unique: "big companies can't make you feel you're wearing a t-shirt with any soul at all."

The designs are inspired by rock music, movies and the street. Grete sums up the company's aims like this: "We want to keep the human touch. Every t-shirt is handmade and just for you. Nobody is going to have another exactly like yours."

'REVOLUTION ALWAYS'

'SKULLY' TEE

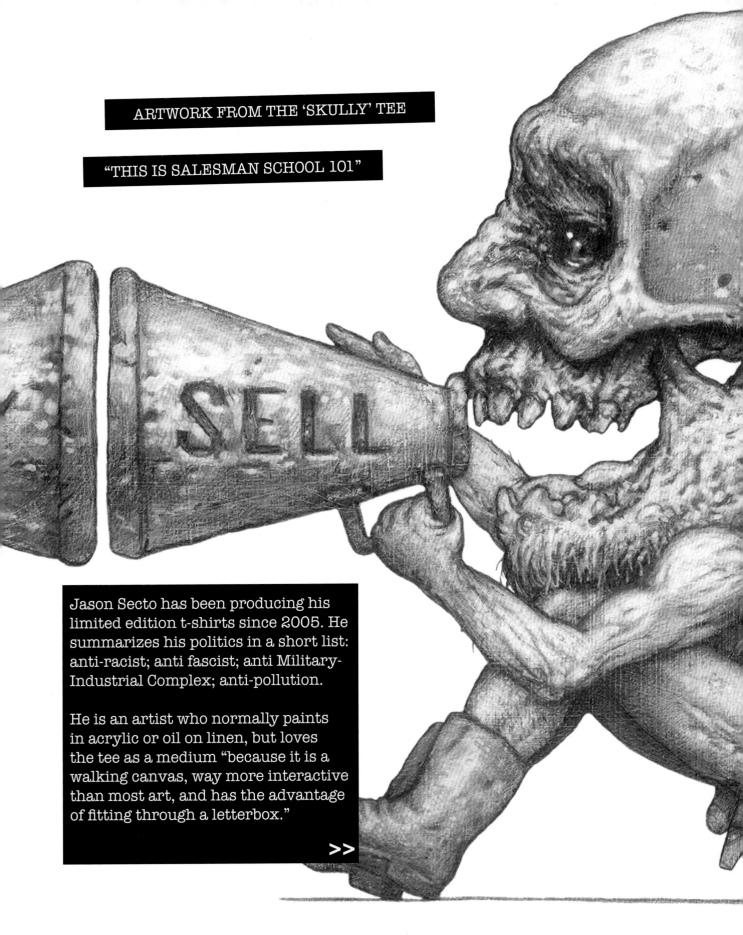

"THIS IS SALESMAN SCHOOL 101"

SELL

Jason Secto has been producing his limited edition t-shirts since 2005. He summarizes his politics in a short list: anti-racist; anti fascist; anti Military-Industrial Complex; anti-pollution.

He is an artist who normally paints in acrylic or oil on linen, but loves the tee as a medium "because it is a walking canvas, way more interactive than most art, and has the advantage of fitting through a letterbox."

>>

His design for the 'Skully' tee is a highly detailed representation of 'Salesman School 101.' The salesmen-in-training are portrayed as primeval, desiccated, ancient imps, engaged in ridiculous activity, shouting in opposition.

Many of Secto's designs make effective use of a mirror image – the opposed pistols with fused barrels, or the two ancient pipe smokers. He is big on his environmental credentials and says "the next stage is going to be fair trade organic cotton!"

'UP IN SMOKE' ARTWORK

'UP IN SMOKE' SHIRT

'SKULLY' TEE

'PEACEMAKER' SHIRT

'PEACEMAKER' ARTWORK

PROGRESSWEAR

'FUNDA/MENTAL' SHIRT

"The masses desperately need to be awakened from their Britney Spears-induced slumber," say Philadelphia-based Progresswear. They are highly political: "we stand for the separation of Church and State; the proper teaching of the theory of evolution in schools; we're against the war in Iraq and the rise of fundamentalism on our own soil."

Progresswear's designs make use of twists of language, smart typography and witty imagery to make their points. They are confident that protest messages on t-shirts can make a difference: "one to five effective and perhaps humorous words on a t-shirt worn by one of our buyers may be read by hundreds, if not thousands, of unsuspecting viewers in a single day. People lost in the minutiae of their lives, chatting away, are suddenly reminded of topics far more serious, that they spend little time thinking about, or avoid thinking about. They find it that bit harder to deny their culpability in enabling the rush to war. LIERAQ will always be a valid slogan, lest we forget."

Progresswear run an ethical outfit and a proportion of the profits from the sale of their LIERAQ t-shirts goes to the Veterans For Peace charity. They are currently polling their buyers on which other organizations they should support in future.

THE 'LIERAQ' SHIRT

'INTELLIGENT DESIGN ISN'T': SHOOTING DOWN

CREATIONISM BY ANOTHER NAME

ANOTHER SHOT OF THE 'LIERAQ' SHIRT

THIS TIME WITH PANTIES

JENKY PRODUCTIONS

THE 'SUFFER EGOCIDE' SHIRT

Jenky Productions "has always been about fun." In 2006 Jenky started out designing shirts "not for a lack of shirt options; rather we wanted to roll up our sleeves and debate about design, ink ourselves while experimenting with printing, and sweat on the sidewalk in Soho trying to sell a few tees." Jenky support fair labor vendors, using vertically-manufactured tees from American Apparel, and printing locally in Brooklyn. They reflect New York's rich urban culture in their work, and their love of, and obsession with, cycling.

THE 'I BIKE NY' SHIRT

HEY PILGRIM!

'BUDDHA QUOTE' SCARF (TO MATCH SHIRT OPPOSITE

AND 'WHAT IS BANGKOK?' SHIRT

Hey Pilgrim!'s 'What is Bangkok?' collection responds to the city where the company is based with a mix of neon colours, faded prints and quotes from Buddha. As well as the 'Buddha Quote' tee opposite, one shirt bears the words "what we think we become" and each neck label is printed with "everything is changeable, everything appears and disappears." The combination of ancient philosophy and rough-edged design answers their question in eclectic style.

The company are based at JJ Market in Bangkok and have been making t-shirts since early 2007. They say that their designs, which are silk screen printed, are inspired by "travel, music, movies and random thoughts on life."

THE 'WISE' SHIRT

'BUDDHA QUOTE' TEE:

HOW CAN ONE EVER KNOW

ANYTHING IF THEY ARE TOO

BUSY THINKING?

CREDITS AND CONTACT DETAILS

2SICKBASTARDS (p66-71)
www.2SICKBASTARDS.com
info@2SICKBASTARDS.com

Adam Hunt for Amnesty (p181-183) see **Goatboy**

Are You Generic? (p184-189)
Okat
www.areyougeneric.org
iamokat@gmail.com

Birdhead Design (p94-95)
Michael Crigler
www.birdheaddesign.com
mc@birdheaddesign.com

Brian Wood Exclusive (p58-65)
www.brianwoodonline.com
info@brianwoodonline.com

Dangerous Breed (p42-45)
www.dangerousbreed.net
info@dangerousbreed.net

District Cotton (p98-99)
www.districtcotton.com

Fat American (p190-197)
All designs by Alex Boeckl except 'Wata Dismal World,'
by Austin Petito
Photographer > Wheat Würtzburger >
www.fieldsandfieldsofwheat.com
www.fatamerican.tv
info@fatamerican.tv

FRESHJIVE (p20-29)
WWW.FRESHJIVE.COM

Goatboy (p176-180)
Adam Hunt
www.goatboy.com.au
adam@goatboy.com.au

Gorilla Riot (p84-91)
www.gorillariot.com
gorillariotinfo@gmail.com

Hans and Fras (p148-149)
www.hansandfras.com
help@hansandfras.com

Hey Pilgrim! (p252-253)
www.heypilgrim.com
pilgrim@heypilgrim.com

Hey! Unite (p114-117)
Matt Genitempo, Britt Knighton, Joel Peel
www.heyunite.com
hey@heyunite.com

HippyTree (p150-151)
PO Box 1137, Hermosa Beach, CA 90254 USA
company founder and creative director: Andrew
Sarnecki
www.hippytree.com
hippytree@gmail.com

Ilk Industries (p208-209)
Designs > Ilk Industries
Photography > IfLooksCouldKill Ltd
www.ilkindustries.com
heythere@ilkindustries.com

Jenky Productions (p250-251)
www.jenkyproductions.com
adam@jenkyproductions.com

John Yates at Alternative Tentacles (p152-154)
www.alternativetentacles.com
mailorder@alternativetentacles.com

John Yates (p152-157)
Stealworks > www.stealworks.com
www.planetoftheyates.com
info@stealworks.com

John Yates for Mighty Healthy (p155-157)
www.mightyhealthynyc.com
info@mightyhealthynyc.com

Katharine E Hamnett Ltd (p122-129)
Photographer > Alex Sturrock
www.katharinehamnett.com
info@katharinehamnett.com

Kindred (p130)
Paul Hunsicker
www.kindredmarket.com
paul@kindredclothiers.com

Kiser (p32-37)
Kiser Barnes
www.kiserny.com
kiser@kiserny.com

Klaus Industries (p232-237)
Grant Davis
www.klausindustries.com
info@klausindustries.com

Kowtow (p198-207)
All designs by Boofa except 'Alice,' by Susie Gibson
www.kowtow.co.nz
info@kowtow.co.nz

Lanzy Clothing Co (p214-217)
Designer > Guojeck Loo
Photographer > Esther Liang
Model > Guojeck Loo
www.iamlanzy.com
info@iamlanzy.com

Maak Eebuh (p18-19)
www.maakeebuh.com
info@maakeebuh.com

Mama (p50-57)
Designs > Mama, Gabriella Davi-Khorasanee
Photographer > Amanda Lopez
www.mamaclothing.com
mama@mamaclothing.com

New Internationalist (p106-107)
www.newint.org
www.newint.com.au/shop/fair-trade.htm
shop@newint.com.au

ORIGIN68 (p108-109)
www.origin68.com
info@origin68.com

Pop Vulture T-Shirt (p92-93)
Samuel Soloff/Pascal Liening
www.popvulturetshirt.com
info@popvulturetshirt.com

Pretty Hammer (p131)
www.prettyhammer.com
info@prettyhammer.com

Progresswear (p246-249)
Photographers > Patrick King (p246) Tony Ward
(p247-249)
www.progresswear.com
info@progresswear.com

Projet M (p146-147)
Photographer > www.ghostlab.fr
www.projet-m.com
contact@projet-m.com

R-ev (p210-213)
Designer > Marek Zanisza a.k.a. Akitoy
www.r-ev.net
marek@r-ev.net

RNDM (p80-81)
Mattias Mattisson – RNDM STRTS
www.rndm.se
sales@rndm.se

Secto (p240-245)
Jason Secto
secret.art.academy@gmail.com

SEEE (p8-15)
www.seee.us

Social Atelier (p72-79)
Designs > Social Atelier
Photographer > John Collazos
www.socialatelier.com
info@socialatelier.com

SOULD (p132-145)
www.SOULD.com
info@SOULD.com

SOY (p158-167)
www.soyclothing.com
jovi@soyclothing.com

Spraygraphic (p82-83)
www.spraygraphic.com
info@spraygraphic.com

Street Attack (p96-97)
Luke Garro
www.streetattack.com
luke@streetattack.com

The Gretest (p238-239)
Designer > Grete Garrido
www.thegretest.com
thegretest@gmail.com

The Loots (p30-31)
www.theloots.com
skops@theloots.com

The Love Movement for Ropeadope (p16-17)
www.timphilly.com
www.ropeadope.com

Tippi Tappi (p118-121)
www.tippitappi.com
info@tippitappi.com

Tonic (p46-49)
www.tonicgen.com
info@tonicgen.com

Too Black Guys (p222-231)
www.nineteen-ninety.com
info@nineteen-ninety.com

Turtlehead (p218-221)
www.turtlehead.ie
keith@turtlehead.ie

Vanguard American (p100-105)
www.vanguardamerican.com

We are Numbers (p174-175)
Photographs > p174: clockwise from top left – No12:
Anonymous shot by The Mofo in London, UK (www.
the-mofo.co.uk)// No14: Anonymous shot by The Mofo
// No09: Olivia shot by The Mofo // No42: Nani at the
'Rio De La Plata' Buenos Aires // No18: Annalisa shot by
The Mofo // No14: see above // No42: see above // No13:
Patricia shot by The Mofo;
p175: No15: Hattie shot by The Mofo
Developer: Twan Verdonck
www.wearenumbers.com
info@wearenumbers.com

Wemoto (p110-113)
Stefan Golz
www.wemoto.de
info@wemoto.de

WRONGWROKS (p168-173)
www.wrongwroks.com
info@wrongwroks.com

You Work For Them (p38-39)
www.youworkforthem.com

Young Lovers (p40-41)
www.younglovers.com.au
lovers@younglovers.com.au

GRAFFITO BOOKS WOULD LIKE TO THANK ALL CONTRIBUTORS.
FOR SUBMISSIONS FOR FUTURE PUBLICATIONS PLEASE EMAIL info@graffitobooks.com